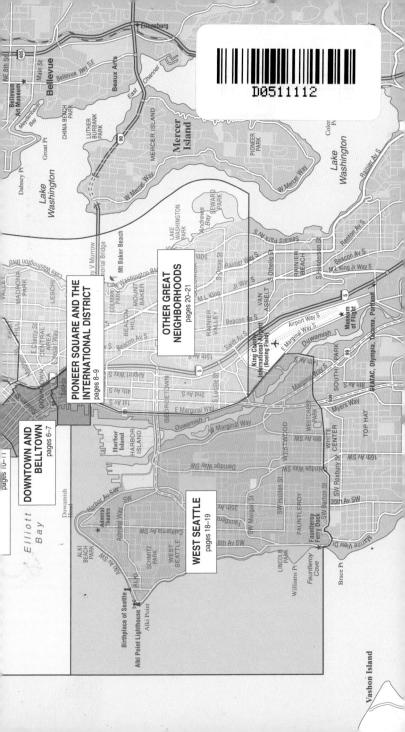

DOWNTOWN AND BELLTOWN
pages 6–7

PIONEER SQUARE AND THE INTERNATIONAL DISTRICT
pages 8–9

OTHER GREAT NEIGHBORHOODS
pages 20–21

WEST SEATTLE
pages 18–19

SEATTLE
smart guide

Contents

Below: the cutting-edge
Seattle Central Library.

Left: floating homes on Lake Union.

Atlas

*Inside Front Cover:
    City Locator
Inside Back Cover:
    Around Seattle*

Below: the pumpkin-carving competition at Fremont's Oktoberfest.

Seattle

Frequently ranked among the country's best places to live, Seattle is a vibrant metropolitan center with world-class arts and entertainment and easy access to nature. With a beautiful setting between the Cascade and Olympic Mountains, with Puget Sound and Lake Washington lapping at its shores, the city has been molded by the rugged landscape that surrounds it.

Destination Facts and Figures

Population: 586,200
Area: 84 sq miles (217 sq km)
Per capita income: $30,306
Annual average precipitation: 37.7ins (957.6mm)
Seattleites (25+) with a Bachelor's degree or higher: 53 percent
Seattleites who are gay, lesbian, or bisexual: 12.9 percent, second only to San Francisco in US

Musicians, Bookworms, and Coffee Drinkers

Seattle offers a good quality of life, with not only spectacular natural environs and a healthy economy, but with a wealth of arts and cultural offerings. There is a thriving theater, music, and film scene. Festivals held throughout the year showcase the talents and unique contributions of the many different cultures that call the Pacific Northwest home. Sporting events are well attended, as fans turn out to support the local teams.

With a well-educated population, it's hardly surprising that Seattle has an excellent library system, and the city's beloved bookstores offer frequent book-readings and author events. The bountiful coffee shops, too, lend themselves to hunkering down over a laptop, discussing liberal politics with friends, or escaping from the rain with a good book.

Outdoor Paradise

The region is a magnet for nature-lovers, with abundant recreational opportunities available year-round. Even around town, the inhabitants are more likely to be sporting Gore-Tex and fleece than suits and ties. Sailors, kayakers, and canoeists are drawn to the beautiful waters of the Puget Sound and the freshwater Lake Union and Lake Washington. In summer you can take the plunge into the cool water, if you dare! And in winter, what better way to liven up your day than to hit the slopes at Snoqualmie Pass for thrilling downhill skiing or snow-boarding the half-pipe? Groomed trails meander through the woods for cross-country skiers and snowshoers, if a quieter pace is more your thing. With its spectacular setting and proximity to water, forests, and mountains, the region is laced with hiking and biking trails that will bring you closer to nature. And a few hours' drive away, eastern Washington has desert-like landscape punctuated by well-irrigated orchards, while the Olympic Peninsula is home to one of the few temperate rainforests in existence.

Diverse Economy

Some of international commerce's best-known names are headquartered in the Seattle area, including software giant Microsoft,

Below: Seattleites in GasWorks Park.

coffee sensation Starbucks, and online retailer Amazon. The long-established Boeing Company moved its headquarters to Chicago, but continues to be a strong presence in the region.

Seattle's strategic location as the closest major port in the lower 48 states to Asia also ensures its prominence in global shipping. Every day huge container ships dock in the Port of Seattle, with massive orange cranes unloading containers full of cars and consumer goods for sale across America, before being loaded back up for the return journey with anything from eastern Washington's famous apples to raw materials such as wood, which grows so abundantly in the Pacific Northwest. Giant cruise ships also dock in Seattle on their route up and down the Pacific.

On the local level, Seattle is experiencing a construction boom since zoning laws have been changed to allow higher-density building, particularly in the South Lake Union, Fremont, and Ballard neighborhoods. South Lake Union is slated to become an even more important area for biomedical research, and is already home to important research institutions such as the Fred Hutchinson Cancer Research Center. Among its other accolades, Seattle is a leader in health care, with some of the finest hospitals and surgeons in the nation.

Highlights

▲ The iconic Space Needle is the centerpiece of the **Seattle Center**, where culture and the arts come together. ▶The proximity to nature means that Seattleites gravitate to **outdoor activities**, from hiking and biking to sailing and skiing.

▶ The city's historic heart is the cobbled, red-brick **Pioneer Square** neighborhood, with art galleries, bookstores, and boutiques.

▲ The city that launched Hendrix and Nirvana to superstardom rocks on every night with a steady stream of **live music**.

▲ In the US **coffee capital**, baristas elevate lattes to a high art form. ▶ Flying fish, floral bouquets, gleaming produce, unique arts and crafts, and delicious ethnic foods epitomize the **Pike Place Market**.

Downtown and Belltown

With a skyline made familiar to millions by the opening credits of the TV series *Frasier*, Downtown Seattle has many features typical of American cities – towering skyscrapers abuzz with commerce, upscale shopping centers and restaurants, splendid theaters – but also the one-of-a-kind Pike Place Market and astonishing views of sparkling Elliott Bay. The waterfront is a hub of maritime activity, from the Washington state ferries that provide service to islands within Puget Sound, to the Seattle Aquarium, and the cruise ship terminal. North of Downtown is the stylish and hip Belltown, with its trendy boutiques and hip bars, clubs, and restaurants.

See Atlas pages 132–136

fantastic details, from the Beaux-Arts **Cobb Building** with the terracotta heads of Indian chiefs to the ornate former **Coliseum Theater** which now houses Banana Republic, to the angular, super-modern **Seattle Central Library** made of steel and glass.

SEE ALSO ARCHITECTURE, P.26, 27; MUSEUMS AND GALLERIES, P.76; MUSIC, P.82; THEATER AND DANCE, P.122, 124

Best Shopping

Big department stores and upscale shopping centers are located on Pine Street. Two department stores predominate: Seattle-based **Nordstrom** ③, with its solid reputation for quality apparel and attentive customer service, and New York-based **Macy's**, which brings national fashions and home furnishings to the Pacific Northwest. Also on Pine is the upscale **Pacific Place** shopping center, and **Westlake Center**, which appeals more to the masses. From the third floor of Westlake Center, you can catch the **Monorail** to the Seattle Center, a fun journey that takes 90 seconds. Branches of many national clothing, shoe, and accessory stores fill the streets around Pine and Pike Streets.

SEE ALSO SHOPPING, P.116, 117

Downtown's Cultural Core

Besides being the business and financial center of the city, Downtown Seattle is also a rich cultural center, home to the world-class **Seattle Symphony** at the elegant **Benaroya Hall** ①, the **Seattle Art Museum** ②, and two historic theaters: the Chinese-themed **5th Avenue Theatre** and the **Paramount Theatre**. One of the pleasures of

walking around Downtown is the varied architecture with

Throughout the year different attractions fill **Westlake Park**, the plaza opposite Westlake Center. From Peruvian pipers to horse-drawn carriages, carrousels, and Christmas celebrations, there's often something to enjoy. Local teens also gather here.

Left: the Seattle waterfront.

underneath the Alaskan Way Viaduct. The working waterfront includes the **Washington State Ferries Terminal** at Pier 52, with regular car and passenger service to Bremerton and Bainbridge Island *(see p.23)*. Pier 54 is home to **Ye Olde Curiosity Shop**, which contains a bizarre array of souvenirs and gifts. From Pier 55 you can catch the water taxi to West Seattle. Farther north at Pier 59 is the **Seattle Aquarium** ⑥, with its touch pools and underwater glass dome. Also fascinating for kids is the **Odyssey Maritime Discovery Center** at Pier 66, which is also the Bell Street Cruise Terminal.
SEE ALSO CHILDREN, P.34, 35; TRANSPORTATION, P.127

Belltown ⑦

Located north of Downtown and south of the Seattle Center, this is a hip neighborhood of high-priced condos, upscale boutiques, and tons of restaurants. Belltown is also home to some of the city's liveliest nightlife, with stylish bars, a few dives, and music clubs. It was here during the 1990s that grunge really took off at classic venues like the Crocodile Café, which closed suddenly in 2007, and the **Moore Theatre**.
SEE ALSO THEATER AND DANCE, P.123

Metro Transit operates a ride-free zone through Downtown, allowing you to move between sights without wearing out your legs or dipping into your wallet, while deep underground is a transit tunnel for easy passage of buses and light rail. The **Waterfront Streetcar Line** (bus 99) provides free service along the waterfront as a temporary replacement for the vintage Trolley service. *See also Transportation, p.126–7.*

Pike Place Market ④

For fresh market produce, beautiful bouquets of seasonal flowers, unique hand-crafted gifts, and inexpensive ethnic food, head to Pike Place Market. Established as a farmers' market in 1907, its continued presence in an area of sky-high real-estate prices is a testament to the vision of

local architect Victor Steinbruck and others who spearheaded a campaign in the late 1960s and early '70s to save the market from demolition.

At the north end of the Market is **Victor Steinbruck Park** ⑤, with gorgeous views across Puget Sound to the Olympic Mountains.
SEE ALSO SHOPPING, P.119

Waterfront

From the Market, the **Pike Street Hillclimb** leads down to the bustling waterfront via a series of stairs and elevators

Right: buskers at Pike Place Market.

Pioneer Square and the International District

South of Downtown, these two adjacent neighborhoods provide distinctly different atmospheres. Historic Pioneer Square was central to the Klondike Gold Rush back in 1897–8, and it has been beautifully preserved as a National Historic District. At night, it's a vibrant scene with many bars and live music. The International District (ID) is a bustling community of Asian restaurants, stores, and businesses. Successive waves of immigration have brought a vibrancy and richness of culture to Seattle.

Pioneer Square

Pioneer Place, with its carved totem poles and lovely iron-and-glass pergola, is a good starting point for exploring this attractive, old-fashioned neighborhood. The sturdy **Pioneer Building** is the meeting point for **Bill Speidel's Underground Tour** ①, a fascinating and irreverent journey back in time through the labyrinthine lower level of Seattle, which was sealed off when engineers raised the streets by one story in the 1890s. Across Yesler Way from Pioneer Place is the Merchant's Café, one of the oldest restaurants in the city.

Heading south on tree-shaded **1st Avenue**, which is lined with galleries, specialist bookstores, and inexpensive restaurants, you'll come to one of the city's favorite spots: the **Elliott Bay Book Com-**

The noisy elevated highway – the **Alaskan Way Viaduct** – that separates Pioneer Square from the waterfront suffered damage in the 2001 Nisqually earthquake. The viaduct needs to be replaced, but no final decision has been agreed as to whether its replacement will be another viaduct, a street-level option, or a tunnel.

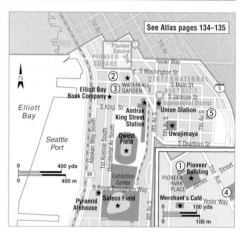

See Atlas pages 134–135

pany. This venerated institution has room after room of new and used books, and their author events are some of the best-attended in town.

Main Street leads north to cobbled **Occidental Park** ②, with its totem poles and a memorial to firefighters. Although attractive, this area has been known as a gathering spot for the local homeless population, who are drawn to the missions and shelters of the neighborhood. Farther up Main at 2nd Avenue is the tranquil and tiny **Waterfall Garden**.

The fascinating **Klondike Gold Rush National Historic**

Park ③ is a must-see to understand the important role that Seattle played as a provisioning stop for the gold rush.

Another piece of the historic puzzle is the elegant **Smith Tower** ④, built in 1914 by typewriter tycoon Lyman Cornelius Smith, at which time it was the tallest building west of the Mississippi. Venture inside to admire the gorgeous lobby; you can ride to an observation deck at the top, which provides impressive views of the Port of Seattle and Pioneer Square.
SEE ALSO ARCHITECTURE, P.26; MUSEUMS AND GALLERIES, P.76, 77; SHOPPING, P.113

Left: red-brick buildings in historic Pioneer Square.

best-value pan-Asian restaurants in town, that also happen to be open the latest (some until 3am). You can certainly get your fix of Chinese dim sum, Japanese sushi, Vietnamese pho, and Korean bokum-bop, but save room for some bubble tea (a tea and tapioca drink). If you want to buy your own food, there's no place better than **Uwajimaya**, a huge supermarket that stocks the freshest fish and seafood, an incredible array of Asian baked goods, and much, much more.

To learn more of the history of the ID and the waves of immigrants who formed the community, visit the **Wing Luke Asian Museum** ⑤ (719 S. King Street; www.wingluke.org; Tue–Sun 10am–5pm; admission charge; bus: 7, 14, 36; map p.135 D2). Named in honor of the late Wing Luke, a Seattle city councilor and the first Asian American to hold elected office in the region, this pan-Asia Pacific American museum, housed in a restored 1910 social center for Asian immigrants, provides valuable insight into community while preserving the rich cultures. SEE ALSO FOOD AND DRINK, P.57; RESTAURANTS, P.104

In both Pioneer Square and the ID it's a good idea to exercise caution at night by not walking alone away from the busy areas.

King Street Station and Sports Central

The Amtrak service up and down the West Coast and to points farther east stops at Seattle's **King Street Station**, which has seen better days. Standing in stark contrast across 4th Avenue is the beautifully restored **Union Station**, which is the home of Sound Transit, the region's commuter rail service.

On any game day you can't fail to notice the hordes of baseball fans streaming southwards to watch the Mariners at **Safeco Field**, or Seahawks fans moving en masse to support their

favorite football team at **Qwest Field**. Lots of them will detour to the bars on the way there or back. **Pyramid Alehouse** (1201 1st Avenue S), one of Seattle's microbreweries, is a popular stop. SEE ALSO SPECTATOR SPORTS, P.120–1

International District

Known as the ID for short, the International District is the site of some of the best-tasting,

Right: a carved totem pole at Pioneer Place.

9

Seattle Center and Lower Queen Anne

The Seattle Center, in the visitor-friendly Lower Queen Anne neighborhood, manages to remain as popular now as it was when it was built for the 1962 World's Fair. While the temporary exhibitions have long since disappeared, Seattle's heavy-hitters of the cultural world – the Seattle Opera, Pacific Northwest Ballet, and Seattle Rep – now make the Center their home. The highlight for many visitors, however, is the iconic Space Needle, with the Frank Gehry-designed Experience Music Project a close second.

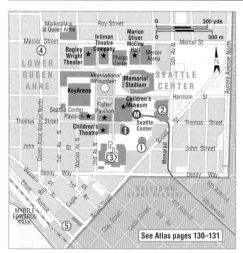

See Atlas pages 130–131

Space Needle

The important cultural hub of the **Seattle Center** lies just north of Belltown, easily accessed from Downtown via buses 3 or 4, or via the monorail from Westlake Center, which makes the 90-second journey every 15 minutes. As it snakes along, interesting vistas of Belltown open up, before the final bend through the Experience Music Project.

As you exit the monorail, the city's icon and most visited sight towers in front of you. Standing at 605ft (185m), the **Space Needle** ① can be seen throughout the city, but it's from the top that the real wow-factor kicks in – the 360-degree viewing deck provides unbelievable views. Just below the observation deck is **Sky City Restaurant**, which revolves once an hour. It has maintained the original 1960s feel, and the food isn't bad either. If you dine there, your elevator ride is free.
SEE ALSO ARCHITECTURE, P.26–7; RESTAURANTS, P.105

Seattle Center Museums

Once you've descended from the lofty heights, you have your choice of unique museums. Paul Allen's **Experience Music Project** (EMP) and **Science Fiction Museum** ② provide an entertaining journey through modern musical history (with a strong focus on the Seattle scene, *see p.83*) and a spooky descent into a brave new world, respectively. The **Pacific Science Center** ③, with its graceful pointed arches and pools of water, holds fascinating exhibits on science and technology, and also has two IMAX theaters. If you have the kids with you, they'll love it, while the younger ones will feel right at home at the **Children's Museum** in the Center House, which is also where the food hall is housed. The Seattle Children's Theatre can also be found here.
SEE ALSO ARCHITECTURE, P.27; CHILDREN, P.34–5; MUSEUMS AND GALLERIES, P.77–9

The Seattle Center holds dozens of festivals throughout the year, including the city's biggest festivals – **Northwest Folk Life Festival** and **Bumbershoot**. It's also the sight of amazing fireworks displays, which shoot off from the Space Needle at the stroke of midnight on New Year's Eve. *See also Festivals, p.52, 53.*

Left: the Space Needle with the Olympic Sculpture Park in the foreground.

hood surrounding it is chock-a-block with restaurants, cafés, and bars (especially along W. Roy, Mercer St, and Queen Anne Avenue N). But there are also important sights away from the Center, including the experimental **On the Boards** organization, which stages some of Seattle's most innovative mixed-media productions.

As Queen Anne slopes down to the water, two parks with breathtaking views come into focus. The Seattle Art Museum's **Olympic Sculpture Park** ⑤ marries large-scale modern sculptures with carefully selected plantings and a superb Puget Sound setting. Linked to it is the long, thin **Myrtle Edwards Park**, tucked between Elliott Bay and the railroad tracks, with a popular walking and cycling path that leads up to a huge grain elevator. Queen Anne Avenue N. extends up the hill to the quieter Upper Queen Anne neighborhood full of Craftsman-style homes, pleasant coffee shops, neighborhood restaurants, and boutiques.

SEE ALSO PARKS, GARDENS, AND BEACHES, P.97–8; THEATER AND DANCE, P.124–5

Center of the Arts and Entertainment

Several high-caliber companies are based at the Seattle Center. The state-of-the-art **Marion Oliver McCaw Hall** is home to the **Seattle Opera**, **Pacific Northwest Ballet**, and the **Seattle International Film Festival (SIFF)**. The Tony-winning **Seattle Rep** performs at the Bagley Wright Theater and the Leo K Theatre, while the **Intiman Theatre Company** and **Seattle Shakespeare Company** also call the Seattle Center home.

But it's not all highbrow. Some of the biggest crowds are drawn to rock and country concerts at the **KeyArena**, when it's not filled with basketball fans supporting the Women's NBA team, the **Seattle Storm**. The 2007–8 season was the final one played here by the Men's NBA team, the **Seattle Sonics**. The team, which was sold to Clay Bennett, has moved to Oklahoma City, much to the chagrin of loyal Sonics fans.

SEE ALSO FILM, P.54; MUSIC, P.82; SPECTATOR SPORTS, P.120; THEATER AND DANCE, P.123, 124, 125

Lower Queen Anne ④

With the number of people who descend on the Seattle Center for cultural events, it's hardly surprising that the Lower Queen Anne neighbor-

Right: the Pacific Science Center is a hit with kids.

Capitol Hill

Tattoos, piercings, dyed hair, and street fashion are ubiquitous in this vibrant, gritty neighborhood of musicians, artists, and students. One of the most densely populated neighborhoods in the state is also home to its largest gay and lesbian populations, and a lively mix of people with progressive politics fill the many bars, restaurants, and clubs, no matter what time of day or night. The main drag is Broadway, where you can people-watch from the sidewalk tables. The Pike-Pine corridor throbs with music from the bars and other venues, especially on weekend nights. This urban neighborhood is just a short walk or bus ride (11, 43, 49) east from Downtown.

Broadway ①

Capitol Hill's main thoroughfare is Broadway, stretching from Pike Street and beyond at the south end to Roy at the north end. On the sidewalk just north of Pine Street (on the east side of the street), is the Jimi Hendrix statue by Darryl Smith, honoring the local rock star who made it big. Opposite is the acclaimed **Seattle Central Community College** and the **Broadway Performance Center**, which puts on plays, dance recitals, and films. A block east of the college is the attractive **Cal Anderson Park**, which provides much-needed outdoor space for this neighborhood of largely apartment- and condo-dwellers. An ambitious construction project on the east side of Broadway at Denny is the future home of the Sound Transit station, scheduled to open in 2016,

which will serve the light-rail extension from Downtown via Capitol Hill to the U-District.

Carry on up Broadway past **Dick's Drive-In**, where a steady stream of customers lines up throughout the day and night for burgers and fries. From here to Roy Street, the street is lined with many affordable restaurants, bars, and unique stores, including **Bailey-Coy Books**, with a

good range of gay literature. In nice weather, diners spill onto

> Capitol Hill is the epicenter of the city's gay, lesbian, bisexual, and transgender community. It tends to be a very relaxed place where it's common to see same-sex couples walking arm-in-arm and smooching, and there's lots of casual cruising, too. *See also Gay and Lesbian, p.58–9.*

Right: a patron of the Capitol Hill bar scene.

Left: edgy Capitol Hill has a lively roster of live music.

North Capitol Hill

The farther north you go, the more elegant the neighborhood becomes. Federal Avenue E is often referred to as **Millionaires' Row** since the homes there are gorgeous, stately, and with a price tag to match. It's in this neighborhood that **St Mark's Cathedral** ④ can be found, with its somewhat austere architecture and impressive organ. Its Men's Choir performs every Sunday evening, with the performances broadcast live on local radio. This is also home to **Volunteer Park**, with its great views, grassy lawns, and delightful Conservatory. Located within the park is the **Seattle Asian Art Museum** ⑤. Just north of the park is **Lakeview Cemetery**, final resting place of many of Seattle's good and great.

SEE ALSO MUSEUMS AND GALLERIES, P.79; PARKS, GARDENS, AND BEACHES, P.98

15th Avenue

This is a quieter part of Capitol Hill, with a small but interesting commercial strip and a mellower vibe than the rest of the neighborhood. There are good cafés, bars, and little stores offering everything from gifts to second-hand clothing.

the sidewalks and music pumps out of the speakers. Embedded in the sidewalks along Broadway are bronze footsteps showing *Dance Steps* (by Jack Mackie). At Roy, turn left and you'll see the **Harvard Exit** ②, a Landmark Theatre known for the grand piano in the lobby and the arthouse films it screens. A little farther down Roy is **Cornish College for the Performing Arts**, which turns out some very accomplished dancers, musicians, and other artists.

SEE ALSO FILM, P.55; SHOPPING, P.112

Pike-Pine Corridor

The two parallel streets of Pine and Pike run eastward from Downtown, crossing over the southern end of Broadway, and are lined with a lot of the hipper bars and clubs, and lots of gay establishments. On Pine, look for **The Egyptian** ③ movie theater on the corner of Harvard Avenue E, the area's other Landmark Theatre that screens some great midnight cult shows. At the beloved **Century Ballroom** you can swing, salsa, tango, or lindy-hop the night away.

Pike Street is bar and restaurant central. The **Elysian Brewing Co.** is famed for its microbrews and burgers, and most nights of the week **Chop Suey** has a line of people waiting to get inside to see the latest live bands; down the street the **Comet Tavern** and **Neumo's** also pull in the music crowds. Lots of new places are popping up around Pike and 12th Street, which is also where you can find the **Northwest Film Forum**. Pike is also sprinkled with small stores selling everything from skateboards to records, furniture to fabric.

SEE ALSO FILM, P.54, 55; MUSIC, P.84; RESTAURANTS, P.106–7

Right: St Mark's Cathedral.

Fremont

Fremont developed its reputation as a free-spirited community back in the 1960s, when low rents attracted artists, students, and the socially minded. Over time, imaginative public art appeared, and the wacky Fremont Solstice Parade gained a dedicated following. Its location on the north bank of the Lake Washington Ship Canal offers easy access to Downtown, and professionals and more affluent residents now number among the local population. The demolition of warehouses for office space brought a corporate feel to the area, but pockets of bohemian charm are easily found, from overflowing gardens to community-spirited coffee shops to the Outdoor Cinema.

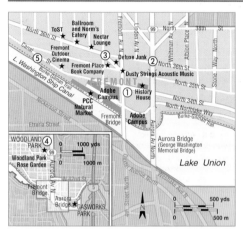

Fremont Avenue North

The main business district of Fremont is the corridor on either side of heavily trafficked Fremont Avenue North, stretching from the bridge up the hill. Peppered in and among the bigger companies, such as **Adobe Systems**, **Getty Images**, and a branch of **Google**, are quirky independent stores including Dusty Strings Acoustic Music Shop, with its hundreds of harps, hammered dulcimers, and guitars, **Deluxe Junk**, which sells some great retro furnishings, and small but lovingly stocked **Fremont Place Book Company**. There is also

a good selection of places to eat, from burgers at the **Red Door Alehouse** to Greek, Thai, and Japanese, while **Simply Desserts** coffee shop provides happy endings.

One of the first sights to catch most visitors' eyes is Fremont's famous public art. On 34th, just north of the Fremont Bridge, Richard Beyer's 1979 sculpture *Waiting for the Interurban* ① occupies the spot of the long-vanished electric Interurban train that provided service between Everett and Seattle. The cast-aluminum sculpture shows a group of passengers waiting for their train, and is fre-

quently regaled with banners, signs, and clothing by local folks. Continue on to 790 N. 34th, where you can learn about local history, including various decorations of Beyer's sculpture, at the **History House**; it also hosts free summer Sunday afternoon concerts in the garden. Another landmark sculpture is the giant *Fremont Troll* ② (1989) lurking under the massive Aurora Bridge on N. 36th. On 36th at the corner of Evanston you'll encounter a 7-ton statue of **Vladimir Lenin** ③, transported to Seattle after the collapse of the Soviet Union, and a block south is a 53ft (16m) *Rocket* (1994) that once blew steam if you fed it quarters.

SEE ALSO BARS, P.32; COFFEE SHOPS, P.40; SHOPPING, P.113, 119

North 36th Street

As you head west along North 36th Street from Fremont Avenue N you'll encounter lots of boutiques, restaurants, bars, and coffee shops. At night, especially weekend nights, this area buzzes with a mid-20s crowd turning out to see live music at **ToST** and **Nectar Lounge**, having a few drinks at the **Ballroom**, sharing the restaurant with pooches at the dog-friendly

Left: Fremont, the 'Center of the Universe'.

At the height of its counter-culture days, this area renamed itself 'The People's Republic of Fremont' and later gave itself the moniker 'Center of the Universe', and, as if to prove the point, there's a signpost at the corner of Fremont Avenue N and Fremont Place showing the distances from Fremont to far-flung places around the globe.

Norm's Eatery and Ale House, or grabbing a coffee at the part solar-powered **Fremont Coffee Company**. It's lively but generally well behaved and not too rowdy. SEE ALSO BARS, P.31; COFFEE SHOPS, P.40; MUSIC, P.84; RESTAURANTS, P.108

North Fremont

The largely residential area north of Fremont, and up a seriously steep hill, is home to the wonderful **Woodland Park Zoo** ④, with its host of fascinating animals, natural habitats, and informative signs and zookeepers. You can happily spend a day here with the kids, or see the lovely **Woodland Park Rose Garden**. In summer, outdoor concerts are held on the grounds. SEE ALSO CHILDREN, P.34; PARKS, GARDENS, AND BEACHES, P.99

Along the Ship Canal

At the intersection of Canal Street and Evanston is the small but perfectly formed **Fremont Canal Park** ⑤, featuring outdoor public art and a nice view of the passing boats. Grab some food from nearby **PCC Natural Market** and have a picnic. From here you can take the paved **Burke-Gilman Trail** west alongside the Ship Canal to Ballard, or east via **Gas-Works Park**, which has fabulous views of Lake Union and Downtown, toward Lake Washington and beyond. SEE ALSO FOOD AND DRINK, P.57; OUTDOOR ACTIVITIES, P.86; PARKS, GARDENS, AND BEACHES, P.95

Fremont Culture

One of the most eagerly anticipated events in the Seattle calendar is the **Fremont Summer Solstice Parade and Street Fair**, which takes place on the weekend nearest the sum-

mer solstice. The local community turns up with extravagant costumes and ornate floats, the zanier the better. Another favorite is the raucous **Fremont Oktoberfest**, held the third weekend in September, with lots of beer and bratwurst. But for a more regular occurrence, the **Fremont Sunday Market** on 34th (between Phinney and Evanston) offers local foods, crafts, clothing, second-hand furniture, and lots of other stuff to root through. On warm summer evenings the **Fremont Outdoor Cinema** at Phinney and N. 34th is the place where locals gather with their chairs, sofas, and blankets to watch a cult or classic movie alfresco. SEE ALSO FESTIVALS, P.52, 53; FILM, P.55; SHOPPING, P.119

Right: Fremont is the unlikely site of this statue of Lenin.

Ballard

Founded by Scandinavian immigrants whose sawmills and shipyards supported the local timber and fishing industries, their rich heritage preserved in Ballard's Scandinavian festivals, a few remaining Nordic businesses, and especially in the Nordic Heritage Museum. In recent years a booming housing market has turned this once quiet outpost into a higher-density neighborhood. At its center, the attractive Ballard Landmark District is great for shopping, eating, and drinking, but the biggest attractions of Ballard are the Locks, where you can watch the ships passing through day or night, and stunning Golden Gardens park.

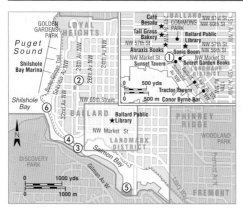

NW Market Street ①

This is the main thoroughfare in Ballard, with the best stores located between 20th and 24th Avenues NW. Take your time browsing the second-hand stores and boutiques, stopping in at **Secret Garden Books** or **Sonic Boom** for books or music, and family-owned **Olsen's Scandinavian Foods** for a taste of Old Ballard with pickled herring or fishcakes. **Vérité Coffee and Cupcake Royale** is perfect for a caffeine-and-sugar fix, or you can opt for **Floating Leaves Tea** and experience an authentic Japanese or Taiwanese tea ceremony.

A block north of Market Street, on 22nd Avenue NW, is the **Ballard Public Library**, an eco-friendly building with a living roof. Diagonally opposite is the **Ballard Commons Park**, with benches, public art, and a skate bowl. A few blocks farther west on 24th are the Tall Grass Bakery and neighboring **Café Besalu**, with their

Away from the rest of the area's sights is the informative **Nordic Heritage Museum** ②, which provides an interesting glimpse into Ballard's Scandinavian roots. Plans are under way to move the museum to a new site at the end of Ballard Avenue that will incorporate Nordic design, heritage, and culture. *See also Museums and Galleries, p.79.*

mouth-watering breads and European pastries. Also on 24th is **Abraxis Books**, with a surprising number of new and used books crammed into the former library.
SEE ALSO COFFEE SHOPS, P.40–41; FOOD AND DRINK, P.57; MUSIC, P.85; SHOPPING, P.112, 113

Ballard Landmark District

The nationally registered historic Ballard Landmark District lies south of Market Street, centered around Ballard Avenue, and is the hub of restaurants, bars, and quirky shops in Ballard. You'll find a wide selection of eateries, from pubs to sophisticated cocktail lounges, from bordello-themed pizza parlors to upscale Italian restaurants, and lots of other places offering decent food and plenty of atmosphere. Ballard has a fun, vibrant nightlife, focused largely on live music and bars. The best-known venues are the farm-themed **Tractor Tavern**, the **Sunset Tavern**, and Irish pub **Conor Byrne**, with a range of live music most nights of the week.

Ballard Avenue is also the site of the Sunday **Farmers' Market**, where you can happily graze and nibble your way from one stall to the next while purchasing local farm-fresh

produce and all sorts of other treats, from cookies or pizza to honey or lavender-scented soaps and lotions. Bring your appetite, and bring a bag to take home your goodies.
SEE ALSO MUSIC, P.84, 85; SHOPPING, P.118

Shilshole Avenue

Just the other side of the Landmark District on Shilshole Avenue you can find the non-gentrified side of Ballard, with its industrial flavor of automotive shops, shipyards, dry docks, welding stores, and marine supply stores, a visible reminder of the area's maritime importance.

The Locks and Salmon Bay

If you need more proof that Ballard (or indeed Seattle) is intrinsically tied to the water, head down to the **Hiram A. Chittenden Locks** ③ on Salmon Bay, a 24/7, 365-day-a-year operation to transport vessels between the freshwater Lake Washington and Lake Union to the saltwater Puget Sound through a sophisticated system of locks. Its other primary task is to allow safe passage for salmon returning to spawn through a system of fish ladders. The Locks is one of the city's major tourist attractions, and on site is a fascinating small museum that documents their construction in 1917 by the US Army Corps of Engineers. There are also images and historical documentation detailing the digging of the

Right: the Hiram A. Chittenden Locks.

Left: Ballard's boats set off for a day on the water.

Lake Washington Ship Canal, which connects Lake Washington and Lake Union to Puget Sound. Before you leave the Locks, take time to stroll through the lovely **Carl S. English, Jr, Botanical Gardens** ④, named after the US Army Corps engineer who designed and tended them.

Fisherman's Terminal ⑤, on the south side of Salmon Bay, is home to Seattle's commercial fishing fleet, with hundreds of large vessels moored here when they're not out plying the waters for salmon, halibut, crab, or other seasonal catches.
SEE ALSO PARKS, GARDENS, AND BEACHES, P.94

Shilshole Bay and Golden Gardens

Cyclists, joggers, and walkers will love the **Burke-Gilman Trail** ⑥, which runs through Ballard to **Shilshole Bay Marina**, home to 1,500 pleasure boats, and eventually terminates at beachfront **Golden Gardens** park, from where you can observe the most glorious sunsets. There are some good seafood restaurants on the waterfront along the way.
SEE ALSO OUTDOOR ACTIVITIES, P.86; PARKS, GARDENS, AND BEACHES, P.95–6

West Seattle

Separated from the rest of the city both geographically and through its relaxed, seaside kind of a vibe, West Seattle occupies a peninsula that you reach either by water taxi from Downtown or by the huge West Seattle Bridge that arches over the Duwamish River and industrial Harbor Island (home to shipyards and container-ship loading facilities). Sandy Alki Beach, with its magnificent views of Puget Sound and the Olympic Mountains, becomes a magnet for Seattleites on any sunny day. The commercial core is the Junction, where stores that have been in business for 40 years rub alongside chic boutiques and stylish restaurants, catering to both young and old.

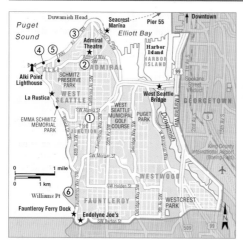

The Junction ①

West Seattle's lively commercial district is centered at the junction of two streets: California and Alaska. California Avenue, in particular, is lined with independent stores, cafés, and restaurants to keep you occupied. **Easy Street Records** is a magnet for music-lovers, with its great selection of CDs and live shows, but if fashion is what you're after, **Clementine** is good for women's shoes, and **Sweetie** has stylish women's wear. When you need to take a break, step into **Coffee to a Tea** for a few of their beautiful mini-cupcakes. If you love seafood, you should check out **Seattle Fish Company**, a terrific fishmonger that stocks all wild fish. If you'd rather let

A fun way to reach West Seattle is by the **Elliott Bay Water Taxi** (from Pier 55 on the Downtown waterfront; $3 each way), which makes the journey to Seacrest Marina in about 12 minutes. From there, it's a short walk to Alki Beach, or you can take the free shuttle van (773) which operates between the Admiral District, Alki Point, and the Junction.

someone else do the work, dive into **Ama Ama** oyster bar. **Shadowland** is another good option for drinks and food.
SEE ALSO BARS, P.33; COFFEE SHOPS, P.41; FOOD AND DRINK, P.57; MUSIC, P.85; SHOPPING, P.115, 116

Admiral District ②

North of the Junction on California is the rolling Admiral District, named for Admiral Way, which climbs the hill from the West Seattle Bridge on the east and slides down to Alki Beach on the west. The district is home to the historic **Admiral Theatre**, which is reviving comedy and cult movies like the *Rocky Horror Picture Show*. A lovely old brick public library is here with some restaurants, including Southwestern-influenced **Mission**, coffeehouses, and West Seattle High School.
SEE ALSO RESTAURANTS, P.111

Alki Beach ③

It was on the windswept shores of what is now Alki Beach that Seattle's pioneers, led by Arthur Denny from the Midwest, first landed and built a community in 1851. After one blustery winter on Alki, however, most of the Denny party moved away from the beach's winds

Left: Alki Point Lighthouse.

(summer tours by appointment; tel: 206-217-6203), established in 1881, with the current lighthouse dating from 1913. A couple of blocks inland is the quaint **Log House Museum** ⑤ (3003 61st Avenue SW; tel: 206-938-5293), located in the former carriage house of the nearby Alki Homestead (now a restaurant), which has an engaging exhibition on the history of West Seattle.

One of the best places to escape the crowds is the lush, verdant **Schmitz Preserve Park**, just east of Alki, with narrow trails that lead through old-growth forest.
SEE ALSO PARKS, GARDENS, AND BEACHES, P.94, 98

Beach Drive

Continue along the waterfront, which becomes Beach Drive, passing beachside homes both extravagant and funky, as well as apartment buildings, **La Rustica** Italian restaurant, and open spaces such as **Emma Schmitz Memorial Park**.

Beach Drive culminates in the lower part of **Lincoln Park** ⑥, designed by the Olmsted brothers (creators of New York's Central Park) and with miles of wooded and waterfront trails, and the heated Colman Pool (open summer). At the south end of Lincoln Park is the **Fauntleroy Ferry Dock**, where boats depart for Vashon Island *(see p.23).*

Beyond Lincoln Park, the main road leads up the hill to the Fauntleroy Business District, the end of the line for the electric streetcar that once connected West Seattle with Downtown. It's home of the aptly named **Endolyne Joe's** restaurant and bar.
SEE ALSO PARKS, GARDENS, AND BEACHES, P.97; RESTAURANTS, P.110

More than half a dozen wall-sized paintings decorate the retail and commercial buildings around the Junction, most depicting the area as it was over a century ago. The best of these is on the wall at California and Edmunds, and looks as if one could walk right into a 19th-century street scene.

---

to the shelter and deeper anchorage of Elliott Bay.

That exodus seems surprising given Alki's current popularity. On warm days Seattle's most famous beach attracts sun-worshippers for beach volleyball, barbecues, romantic sunset strolls, rollerblading or bike-riding along the well-worn path. Even on cooler days, Alki is a wonderful place for a stroll under swirling clouds and squawking seagulls. If the

wind and rain pick up, the area also offers plenty of shelter and places to eat, ranging from bakeries and delis to seafood restaurants with awesome views.

The oldest landmark here is the **Birthplace of Seattle Monument** ④, a concrete column on 63rd Avenue SW and Alki Avenue that was presented to the city in 1905 by Arthur Denny's daughter. Other historical sights include the **Alki Point Lighthouse**

Right: the Birthplace of Seattle Monument at Alki Beach.

19

Other Great Neighborhoods

Seattle is made up of many unique neighborhoods with well-defined identities. Just northeast of Downtown is South Lake Union, which is undergoing a huge transformation. The University District swarms with students, while quieter Wallingford is populated with young couples and families. Some of the most exciting neighborhoods are in South Seattle: lively Columbia City with its restaurants, galleries, and new light rail link to Downtown, and artsy Georgetown, where studios and bars occupy disused warehouses.

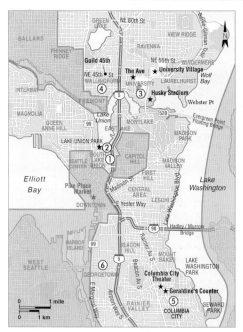

South Lake Union ①

Changes to the zoning have led to an explosion in development of this neighborhood, with the once low-rise wasteland of parking lots being replaced by a high-density neighborhood with mixed-use multi-story buildings, upscale retail space, and huge expansion for biomed-ical research facilities. The development has been led by Microsoft co-founder Paul Allen and his Vulcan Group. The **South Lake Union Discovery Center** at 101 Westlake provides insight into this changing neighborhood.

In 2007 Metro Transit inaugurated the electric **South Lake Union Streetcar**, which links Downtown with South Lake Union, as far as the **Fred Hutchinson Cancer Research Center** on Fairview.

Lake Union Park, due to be completed in 2010, is already bringing accessible lakefront recreation to the public, with great views of the sailboats and seaplanes. Adjacent to the park is the beloved **Center for Wooden Boats** ②, a gem of a living museum in this city that values its maritime heritage.
SEE ALSO INDUSTRY, P.74; MUSEUMS AND GALLERIES, P.79–80; PARKS, GARDENS, AND BEACHES, P.96–7

University District and Wallingford

The U-District lies north of the Lake Washington Ship Canal and is bordered to the east by Lake Washington and to the west by Interstate 5. Mainly populated by students, this neighborhood is centered around the **University of Washington** (UW) ③, which contains a number of points of interest. The attractive campus with grassy lawns, cherry trees, and brick buildings, is home to the **Henry Art Gallery** and the **Burke Museum of Natural History and Culture**, the stately **Suzallo Library** with its stained-glass windows, as well as

Left: a café in Columbia City.

A plethora of cultural events takes place at the University of Washington throughout the year, from classical concerts to big-name author readings to social commentators. Events are announced on the excellent university radio station KUOW 94.9 FM, in the local newspapers, and on the Campus Events Calendar: www.washington.edu/visit/events

Husky Stadium, the home of the Huskies football team.

The main street for hanging out in the U-District is **The Ave**, aka University Way. Along here are tons of small and inexpensive eateries, student bars, and funky little stores, as well as the impressively stocked **University Bookstore**. Opposite is the **Varsity**, one of the historic movie theaters in the neighborhood; another is **The Neptune** on NE 45th, the other main drag through the U-District. If you follow 45th east down the hill, you'll arrive at **University Village**, a swanky outdoor shopping center.

NE 45th west leads across I-5 to the laid-back residential neighborhood of **Wallingford** ④, with a small shopping and dining district along NE 45th. Some of its highlights include the pink **Guild 45th** movie theater, cafés, intimate restaurants, and the **Wallingford Center** with eclectic stores in an old school building.
SEE ALSO FILM, P.55; MUSEUMS AND GALLERIES, P.79, 80; SHOPPING, P.113–14, 117; SPECTATOR SPORTS, P.121

Columbia City ⑤

South Seattle's Columbia City in the Rainier Valley is a fun place to visit, whether for breakfast at **Geraldine's Counter**, to load up with fresh food at the **Farmers' Market**, to catch an evening of burlesque at the **Columbia City Theater**, or to have a

meal at one of the quality restaurants. The hub of cafés, galleries, and restaurants is along Rainier Avenue, south from its intersection with Columbia Way. In late 2009 the light rail link between Sea-Tac International Airport and Downtown will be complete, making Columbia City even more accessible.
SEE ALSO RESTAURANTS, P.111; SHOPPING, P.119; THEATER AND DANCE, P.125

Georgetown ⑥

Occupying an industrial area in South Seattle, hemmed in to the east by Interstate 5 and to the south by Boeing Field, this unlikely area of warehouses, railroad tracks, and industrial wasteland is experiencing an urban renaissance. Attracted by low rents, artists, bars, and galleries have moved in. Most of the best hangouts are located along **Airport Way South**, including Georgetown Liquor Company (at 5501-B) with vegetarian and vegan food, Jules Maes Saloon (5919) with live rockabilly, soul, and rock music, and biker bar Smartypants (6017). **Stellar Pizza** dishes up killer pizza and retro ambience.
SEE ALSO RESTAURANTS, P.111

Left: the University of Washington campus.

Greater Seattle Area

Seattle lies at the center of a large metropolitan area of more than 3.5 million residents, stretching along Interstate 5 from Everett in the north to the state capital Olympia in the south, and from the bucolic Puget Sound islands of Vashon and Bainbridge in the west to the Eastside conurbation of Bellevue, Kirkland, and Redmond on the eastern shores of Lake Washington. Surrounded by snow-capped mountains and sparkling waters, the Greater Seattle Area offers plenty of museums and galleries, antiques shopping, picturesque historic centers, relaxing island getaways, and many more attractions for visitors to explore in easy day trips. *See also Excursions, p.46–51.*

North Sound

The affluent waterfront community of **Edmonds** is home to antiques stores and seafood restaurants, as well as celebrity travel writer and broadcaster Rick Steeves. Edmonds's ferry terminal provides service to Kingston on the Olympic Peninsula.

Farther north is **Everett** ①, the county seat of Snohomish County and home to a US Naval Station, as well as Boeing's assembly plant for the 747, 767, 777, and the new Dreamliner 787.

SEE ALSO INDUSTRY, P.74

Eastside

The Eastside is a lush location of big homes, fine wineries and high-tech companies. **Kirkland**, **Bellevue**, and **Redmond** are the main population centers. Well-heeled Kirkland occupies an enviable setting along the shore of Lake Washington; its attractive center is full of upscale stores and restaurants. It stands in stark contrast to Bellevue, the largest center on the Eastside. This slick, high-rise, corporate city is full of high-end hotels, conference centers, and shopping, especially at

Washington State Tourism is a good source of information for learning more about these destinations. You can contact them by phone at tel: 1-800 544-1800, or go online to www.experiencewa.com

Bellevue Square (NE 8th and Bellevue Way). Farther east is Redmond, best-known for Microsoft HQ, but it also features the huge **Marymoor Park** ② (6046 W. Lake Sammamish Parkway NE) and the carefully planned Redmond Town Center, where hotels, restaurants, and stores are all within easy walking distance.

One of the nicest Eastside getaways is **Woodinville**, where you can indulge in an afternoon of wine-tasting and music at **Chateau Ste Michelle** (14111 NE 145th Street; tel: 425-415-3300; www.ste-michelle.com) or one of many other wineries here.

South Sound

The I 5 corridor south of Seattle is lined with suburbs, from **Des Moines** with a busy marina and popular Redondo Beach, to **Federal Way** – the corporate home of both wood-and-paper giant Weyerhaeuser and Christian nonprofit World Vision, to **Auburn**,

At the southern end of Puget Sound is the state capital, **Olympia** ④. Tours of the imposing domed Legislative Building are offered daily (tel: 360-902 8889; www.ga.wa.gov/visitor). Olympia has a good underground music scene, thanks in part to influences from nearby Evergreen College, and one of the state's best farmers' markets, located on the waterfront.

Islands

Just a 20-minute journey from West Seattle's Fauntleroy Ferry Dock, **Vashon Island** ⑤ is a charming rural area far from the rush of city life. Many residents farm as a hobby and make the daily commute to Seattle or Tacoma via ferry.

One of the easiest getaways from Seattle, **Bainbridge Island** ⑥ is a 35-minute ferry ride from the Seattle Waterfront's Pier 52. **Winslow** is the cute little town on the other side of the crossing, with a few stores and restaurants to keep you busy. Or you can visit the **Bainbridge Island Vineyards and Winery** (8989 Day Road E; tel: 206-842-9463; www.bainbridgevineyards.com), one of Puget Sound's easily accessible wineries.

SEE ALSO TRANSPORTATION, P.127

with its small-town feel and farm-equipment stores.

Tacoma ③ is the state's third-largest city, with almost 200,000 people, a thriving port on Commencement Bay, and vibrant arts scene spearheaded by the **Broadway Center for the Performing Arts** (901 Broadway; tel: 253-591-5890; www.broadwaycenter.org), which stages shows in the historic Pantages and Rialto Theaters. Pacific Avenue is a cultural hub, with a branch of the University of Washington, the restored Beaux-Arts Union Station (now a Federal courthouse), the informative **Washington State History Museum** (1911 Pacific Ave; tel: 888-238-4373; www.wshs.org), and the **Tacoma Art Museum** (1701 Pacific Ave; tel: 253-272-4258). The dazzling Dale Chihuly Bridge of Glass, filled with whirling, swirling, beautiful glass objects by the acclaimed local artist, connects Pacific Avenue with the fabulous **Museum of Glass** below (1801 Dock Street; tel: 253-284-4750). Downtown is also full of historic buildings, including the stunning Pantages Theater at Two. Other must-sees in Tacoma are the path along Ruston Way, which affords wonderful views of Commencement Bay, and Point Defiance Park, with its wooded 5-mile (8km) drive, pebbly beaches, and delightful **Point Defiance Zoo and Aquarium** (tel: 253-404-3678; www.pdza.org).

A–Z

In the following section Seattle's attractions and services are organized by theme, under alphabetical headings. Items that link to another theme are cross-referenced. All sights that are plotted on the atlas section at the end of the book are given a page number and grid reference.

Architecture

Even with its relatively short history, Seattle has a range of architectural styles that mark the different stages in its evolution, from early red-brick buildings in the Pioneer Square neighborhood and ornate Art Deco Downtown office buildings to the '60s retro look of the Seattle Center. In the '90s Frank Gehry's design for the Experience Music Project focused international attention on Seattle, and the cutting-edge Seattle Central Library, designed by Rem Koolhaas, draws admirers from far and wide. A sampling of the city's architectural highlights is presented here, in date order.

Cobb Building (1910)

1305 4th Avenue, Downtown; bus: 1, 7, 16; map p.133 D2
Listed on the National Register of Historic Places, this Beaux-Arts building was designed by the New York firm of Howells & Stokes as a medical-dental building, attested to by the relief of Hippocrates above the entrance. Besides the classical proportions, there are ornate cartouches and detailed terracotta heads of Indian chiefs along the upper stories. It now houses luxury apartments.

Smith Tower (1914)

506 2nd Avenue, Pioneer Square; tel: 206-622-4004; www.smithtower.com; Apr–Oct: daily 10am–sunset, Nov–Mar: Sat–Sun 10am–3.30pm; admission charge (for tower); bus: 3, 16, 99; map p.133 B4
Nowadays Seattle's oldest skyscraper is dwarfed by its neighbors, but at the time of its construction it was the tallest building west of the Mississippi. The lobby is a vision of Mexican onyx, with the original brass and copper Otis elevators still in use. You

can ride to the top to visit the **Chinese Room** with its elaborately carved ceiling and the small observation deck that provides good views of Pioneer Square and the port.

Coliseum Theater (1916)

500 Pike Street, Downtown; bus: 10, 11, 49; map p.133 D3
Now home to a branch of the retail clothing chain Banana Republic, Seattle's first movie theater was designed by B. Marcus Priteca and showed movies until the 1970s. After standing vacant for years, the building was renovated in 1995. Most of the ornate interior decoration is long

since gone, but there is some beautiful plasterwork and domed ceilings, and a glorious neoclassical facade.

Seattle Tower (1929)

1218 3rd Avenue, Downtown; bus: 1, 7, 16; map p.133 D2
You could easily walk right by this 27-story Art Deco tower designed by Albertson, Wilson & Richardson without noticing it, but if you look up, you'll notice the elegantly tapered roofline and the stylized trees at the very top. Take a look inside at one of the most ornate lobbies in town.

Space Needle (1962)

400 Broad Street, Seattle Center; tel: 206-905-2100; www.space needle.com; Sun–Thur 9am–11pm, Fri–Sat 9am–midnight; admission charge; bus: 3, 4, 16; map p.130 B2
The 605-ft (184-m) tall Space Needle is the most recognizable symbol of Seattle. Built in 1962 for the World's Fair, it has remained Seattle's most

Left: looking up at the iconic Space Needle.

Experience Music Project (1996)

325 5th Avenue N, Seattle Center; tel: 206-367-5483; www.empsfm.org; daily 10am–5pm; admission charge; bus: 3, 4, 16; map p.130 B2
Frank Gehry's postmodern design is a multicolored, crumpled, gleaming, amorphous structure located at the Seattle Center. It was built over and around the existing monorail tracks from the 1962 World's Fair, creating a tunnel effect.
SEE ALSO MUSEUMS AND GALLERIES, P.77–8

Seattle Central Library (2004)

1000 4th Avenue, Downtown; tel: 206-386-4636; www.spl.org; Mon–Thur 10am–8pm, Fri–Sat 10am–6pm, Sun noon–6pm; bus: 2, 10, 49; map p.133 D1
Seattle's spectacular Central Library, designed by Dutch architect Rem Koolhaas, garnered international acclaim for its cutting-edge design. The steel-and-glass exterior, jutting out at unexpected angles over the sidewalk and into the sky, allows incredible light inside, giving the space the feel of a giant atrium enclosed within diamond-shaped panes of glass.

The **Seattle Architecture Foundation** puts on exhibitions related to local architecture, and offers a variety of guided tours. You can find them in Rainier Square (in the base of the Rainier Tower) at 1333 5th Avenue; tel: 206-667-9184; www.seattlearchitecture.org.

popular attraction and now welcomes more than 1 million visitors a year. The graceful white structure is topped by a 360-degree viewing platform, with fantastic views that really orientate you geographically to the snow-capped mountains of the Olympics and the Cascades, as well as the glistening waters of the Puget Sound, Lake Union, and Lake Washington. Just below the platform is the revolving **Sky City Restaurant**.
SEE ALSO RESTAURANTS, P.105

Rainier Tower (1979)

1301 5th Avenue, Downtown; bus: 1, 7, 16; map p.133 D2
Seattle-born architect Minoru Yamasaki designed this perfectly proportioned white tower in 1979. Within the flared base is an upscale shopping arcade and restaurants, while the 40-story tower houses office space.
SEE ALSO SHOPPING, P.117

Bars

Seattle's bar scene ranges from urbane, sophisticated wine bars to wild live-music venues, and just about everything between. Downtown and Belltown have upscale lounges, while Pioneer Square is more rough and ready, with patrons hopping from bar to bar to see the live music offered at many. Capitol Hill attracts a young hip crowd and also has a high concentration of gay bars. College kids and young professionals flock to Fremont and lower Queen Anne, while Ballard and West Seattle have a more grown-up vibe. *See also Gay and Lesbian, p.58–9; Music, p.82–5;* for bars that are food destinations, *see also Restaurants, p.100–111.*

Downtown and Belltown

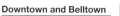

Alibi Room
85 Pike Place; tel: 206-623-3180; www.seattlealibi.com; daily 4pm–2am; bus: 10, 15, 18; map p.136 B3
Located on an alley that curves around Pike Place Market, it feels like you could be wandering through a cobbled European street as you enter this cool bar, which serves good cocktails and appetizers to share.

Cyclops Café & Lounge
2421 1st Avenue; tel: 206-441-1677; www.cyclopsseattle.com; Mon–Thur 5–11pm, Sat 4pm–midnight, Sun 4–10pm; bus: 15, 18, 21; map p.132 B4
Hip retro décor distinguishes

The legal drinking age in the US is 21, and you may be asked to prove your age by showing picture ID (driver's license or passport). Because the laws are so stringent, and the fines so heavy, it's not uncommon for even 35- or 40-year-olds to be 'carded.' Most bars open their doors between 3 and 5pm, and stop serving at 2am.

this noisy but fun café and lounge with velvet paintings and a great happy hour from 3–6pm. The cocktails are generous, and the food is good-sized too, and service is friendly.

Kells Irish Pub
1916 Post Alley; tel: 206-728-1916; www.kellsirish.com; daily 11.30am–late; bus: 10, 15, 18; map p.136 A2
This Irish pub serves Guinness and Harp, plus a great selection of traditional Irish fare, from potato farls and soda bread to steak and kidney pie. Frequent live music.

Lava Lounge
2226 2nd Avenue; tel: 206-441-5660; daily 3pm–2am; bus: 13, 15, 18; map p.132 C3
This kitsch tiki-style lounge serves cheap and strong drinks. There are DJs spinning an eclectic mix, as well as a jukebox, pinball, and shuffleboard.

Two Bells Tavern
2313 4th Avenue; tel: 206-441-3050; daily 11am–2am; bus: 1, 2, 13; map p.132 B4
This old-school pub is one of the few remaining such establishments in swanky Belltown, with friendly ser-

Left and below: relax with a beer at the friendly Two Bells Tavern in Belltown.

21; map p.134 B3

Established in 1892, the Central Saloon stakes its claim as Seattle's oldest saloon. There's a good selection of draft and bottled beers, plus cider and some local wines, and a menu that features Reubens (pastrami, mustard, swiss cheese), BLTs, juicy burgers, and ribs. You can catch mostly local rock bands here seven nights a week.

Owl 'N Thistle

808 Post Avenue; tel: 206-621-7777; www.owlnthistle.com; daily 11am–2am; bus: 15, 18, 21; map p.134 B4

This down-to-earth Irish pub has a full bar and serves good Guinness and Guinness beef stew. Irish bands and other bands playing an array of eclectic music are on stage here nightly.

Pioneer Square Saloon

77 Yesler Way; tel: 206-628-6444; daily noon–2am; bus: 15, 18, 21; map p.134 B4

Come for the beer, with more than a dozen microbrews on tap, at this old-style drinking hole which is a welcome change from some of the clubbier bars in Pioneer Square. You can play billiards

vice and some tasty burgers and vegetarian choices. There are occasional bands, but basically people just come to talk with friends over beers.

White Horse Trading Company

1908 Post Alley; tel: 206-441-7767; Mon–Wed 4pm–midnight, Thur–Sat 4pm–2am; bus: 10, 15, 18; map p.136 B2

Step into a little corner of England at this cozy pub with its wooden tables, small fireplace, and convivial owner. Good place to settle in for a few beers among British memorabilia.

Tons of bars in Seattle offer **happy-hour discounts**, with a few bucks off appetizers or small plates, and seriously discounted drinks. Hours vary, but usually fall somewhere between 4 and 7pm weekdays. This is a great way to fill up on inexpensive food and start your evening without breaking the bank.

Pioneer Square and the International District

Central Saloon

207 1st Avenue S; tel: 206-622-0209; www.centralsaloon.com; daily 11.30am–2am; bus: 15, 18,

Left: 22 Doors bar staff and street sign.

tables. Clean, minimalistic, and serving good modern American bar food that's well priced. Moxie's happy hour is later than most, from 8–10pm.

Ozzie's Roadhouse

105 W. Mercer Street; tel: 206-284-4618; daily 8am–2am; bus: 1, 2, 13

Pool tables, karaoke, and a crowd of young people on the sidewalk, this dark and always crowded venue pulls the punters in nightly. They serve food, but it's better enjoyed as a drinking hole at night.

The Sitting Room

108 W. Roy Street; tel: 206-285-2830; Sun, Tue–Wed 5pm–midnight, Thur–Sat 5pm–2am; bus: 1, 2, 8

This upscale European-style lounge is a cut above many others, with very good bar food including delicious cheeses, salamis, and pates, and a decent wine selection in addition to a full bar.

Capitol Hill

22 Doors

405 15th Avenue E; tel: 206-324-6406; daily 5pm–2am; bus: 10

Named for the 22 doors that feature in the decoration, including the bar itself (watch out for the doorknobs), this mellow bar/restaurant is good for a romantic evening over a few glasses of wine and some steamed mussels. Small outdoor patio. Or come weekend mornings for brunch (10am–3pm) with a bloody Mary.

Barça

1510 11th Avenue; tel: 206-325-8263; www.barcaseattle.com; daily 5pm–2am; bus: 11, 49

Packed with beautiful young things, this busy cocktail lounge has a cosmopolitan feel about it. It positively

or watch sports on TV, and there's an outside seating area, too.

Seattle Center and Lower Queen Anne

Jabu's Pub

515 Queen Anne Avenue N; tel: 206-284-9093; bus: 1, 2, 15; map p.130 A3

This neighborhood pub close to Seattle Center offers a great selection of beers as well as a full bar, and has theme nights that include

bingo and beer pong (a drinking game involving tennis balls). There's a pool table and TVs, and occasional DJs spinning tunes.

Moxie

530 1st Avenue; tel: 206-283-6614; www.moxieseattle.com; daily 5pm–2am; bus: 1, 2, 15; map p.130 A3

Moxie is a modern Queen Anne bar and restaurant. The bar area at the front is stylish, and towards the back there's a cozy room with small

It's really hard to find parking in Belltown, lower Queen Anne, and Capitol Hill in particular, so you're much better off taking a Metro bus or taxi. If you do take the car, have a designated driver who won't be drinking.

buzzes with life on weekend nights, where the music and conversation rise to a crescendo, and you might need to reach for another pricey drink to whet your whistle. Check out the lavish restrooms.

Bleu
202 Broadway E; tel: 206-329-3087; Mon–Tue 5pm–2am, Wed–Sun noon–2am; bus: 8, 43, 49
Cozy curtained hideaways and a huge list of inventive cocktails are just two of the attractions at this little Broadway bar, which also serves heaping portions of comfort food like mac and cheese.

Capitol Club
414 E. Pine Street; tel: 206-325-2149; www.thecapitolclub.net; daily 5pm–2am; bus: 10, 12, 14
The Capitol Club has a classy Moroccan theme, with throw pillows, low tables, and a feeling of lavishness. Exotic drinks, deliciously flavored food, and a great upstairs deck.

Comet Tavern
922 E. Pike Street; tel: 206-322-9272; daily noon–2am; bus: 11, 49
Capitol Hill's favorite rock 'n' roll dive bar.
SEE ALSO MUSIC, P.84

Satellite Lounge
1118 E. Pike Street; tel: 206-324-4019; daily 3pm–2am; bus: 10, 11
This small but friendly bar attracts a diverse, offbeat

crowd with its jukebox, good-value drinks, and pretty good food, including vegetarian options. Interesting artwork adorns the walls.

Summit Public House
601 Summit Avenue E; tel: 206-324-7611; www.summitpublic house.com; daily 4pm–2am; bus: 14
Down-to-earth neighborhood pub that shows big sports events (soccer is big) while not being a sports pub per se. Pool table, simple pub grub, outdoor tables, and the occasional barbecue in warm weather.

Fremont

Ballroom
456 N. 36th Street; tel: 206-634-2575; www.ballroomfremont.com; daily 4pm–2am; bus: 28
The Ballroom caters to a young crowd, who come to socialize, drink, eat pizza,

and shoot pool at one of many pool tables. Sultry red décor and paper lamp-shades, with large screens for sports. Outside there's a big, welcoming patio with a fire pit. DJs Thursday through Saturday.

Brouwers
400 N. 35th Street; tel: 206-267-2437; www.brouwerscafe.com; daily 11am–2am; bus: 28
A replica of Brussels's Mannekin-Pis greets you as you enter this large Belgian-inspired bar with its 60 taps and 200 bottles, including Bavik, Chimay, Leffe, and Stella Artois. The stone-rendered walls and cross and skull lend a Goth/medieval feel. Steamed mussels and hearty sausages feature on the menu.

Dad Watsons
3601 Fremont Avenue N; tel: 206-632-6505; www.mcmenamins.com;

B

If beer is your thing, get over to Hale's Brewery in Fremont at 4301 Leary Way NW *(see below)* and take a self-guided tour and then relax with a cold, handcrafted ale.

Mon–Thur 11.30am–1am, Fri–Sat 11.30am–2am, Sun 11.30am–midnight; bus: 28, 82 Part of the Portland-based McMenamins, Dad Watsons is a family-friendly place with a curving bar that's separated off by a railing. Good food and a great range of ales, including seasonal ales. Hammerhead and Terminator Stout are always available.

Hale's Brewery & Pub
4301 Leary Way NW; tel: 206-782-0737; www.halesales.com; Mon–Thur 11am–10pm, Fri 11am–11pm, Sat 9am–11pm, Sun 9am–10pm; bus: 28, 46 The pub for Hale's Brewery serves lighter beers in the summer, including Drawbridge Blonde and Red Menace Big Amber, while more substantial winter offerings include Wee Heavy Winter Ale and Irish Style Nut Brown Ale. Their menu includes sandwiches, salads, pizzas, and burgers.

Red Door Alehouse
3401 Evanston Avenue N; tel: 206-547-7521; www.reddoorseattle.com; daily 11am–2am; bus: 28, 31, 46 The large sun deck is a great place for a cold Northwest microbrew and one of the great burgers on any warm day. This central Fremont location keeps the Red Door hopping, from lunchtime to late night.

Ballard

Bal-Mar
5449 Ballard Avenue NW; tel: 206-297-0500; www.thebalmar.com; daily 5pm–2am; bus: 44, 46 With its high ceilings, red-brick walls, metal staircase, and subdued lighting, Bal-Mar is a sophisticated and spacious bar. Happy-hour snacks and drinks are good value. The vibe is mellow, the clientele relaxed.

Hattie's Hat
5231 Ballard Avenue NW; tel: 206-784-0175; www.hattieshat.com; Mon–Fri 11am–2am, Sat–Sun 9am–2am; bus: 44, 46 With a huge Victorian bar dating from 1904, this kitschy favorite pulls in skater boys and rockers for cheap drinks and comfort food. A giant mural lines one wall, and the others are plastered with old prints. Friendly service. Great for mac and cheese or a scrummy portobello mushroom sandwich at 1am.

Jolly Roger Taproom
1514 NW Leary Way; tel: 206-782-6181; www.maritimebrewery.

Left and below: Fremont's popular Red Door Alehouse.

themed bar has two. In among the giant stuffed marlin and eight-person skull suspended from the ceiling are a bunch of flat-screen TVs showing sports. Wings and chilli mac are among the pub grub. Popular with 20- to 30-year-olds.

West Seattle

Ama Ama
Oyster Bar & Grill
4752 California Avenue SW; tel: 206-937-1514; www.ama-amaseattle.com; daily 4pm–1am; bus: 22

Enjoy oysters, mussels, or scallops with your drinks at beautifully designed Ama Ama, with its Far Eastern flair. Good selection of wine, and full meals are available, too. They also serve weekend brunch from 10am–2pm.

Shadowland
4458 California Avenue SW; tel: 206-420-3817; www.shadowlandwest.com; daily 4pm–2am; bus: 55, 58

A dark interior, with wooden floors and a streamlined bar,

Smoking is banned in all bars and other public places in Seattle. According to the law, you're not permitted to smoke within 25ft (7.6m) of a door or window, though you'll often see groups of smokers standing right outside the door (until someone complains loudly enough).

greet you at stylish Shadowland, where you can enjoy a smooth tangerine cosmo or smoky Martini with cosmopolitan nibbles, from Scotch eggs to beef carpaccio.

West 5
4539 California Avenue SW; tel: 206-935-1966; www.west five.com; Sun–Thur 11am–midnight, Fri–Sat 11am–1am; bus: 55, 85

This lounge in the center of West Seattle's Junction district specializes in Martinis (try the exotic Chartreuse Martini) and rum-based drinks, in addition to having a full bar and good selection of beers. Their food is appealing, whether appetizers or full meals.

ypguides.net; Mon–Thur 11am–11pm, Fri–Sat 11am–midnight, Sun noon–9pm; bus: 28, 46

The old-style pub of the Maritime Brewery has, not surprisingly, a maritime theme. Their pilsner and pale ale are to die for, and the food is also good – burgers, fish and chips, and the like.

Lock n' Keel
5144 Ballard Avenue NW; tel: 206-781-9092; daily 11am–2am; bus: 44, 46

It's hard to find a pool table in Ballard, and this maritime-

Children

Seattle has some fun, educational, and adventurous activities for kids and their parents. Top of the list are the Children's Museum and the Pacific Science Center, where kids can explore the world around them through vibrant interactive displays, the wonderful Woodland Park Zoo with its natural habitats for the animals, and Ride the Ducks – an amphibious WWII vehicle that tours the city's roadways and waterways and that's fun for kids of all ages. The city is also well served by family-friendly parks, playgrounds, and beaches; for more information *see also Parks, Gardens and Beaches, p.94–9.*

Animals and Sealife

Seattle Aquarium
Pier 59, Downtown; tel: 206-386-4300; www.seattleaquarium.org; daily 9.30am–5pm; admission charge; bus: 99; map p.132 C2
Check out a giant Pacific octopus, watch sharks and sturgeons circling around you in the cool Underwater Dome, or touch a starfish or sea cucumber in a touch pool. Throughout the day naturalists give talks, and even the scuba-divers who enter the tanks to feed the fish are fitted with microphones. One of the favorite areas is the marine mammal exhibit with its entertaining seals and sea lions.

Woodland Park Zoo
Aurora Avenue N/N. 59th Street, Fremont; tel: 206-684-4800; www.zoo.org; May–Sept: daily 9.30am–6pm, Oct–Apr: 9.30am–4pm; admission charge; bus: 5
Over 300 animal species can be seen in this 92-acre (37-hectare) zoo with six award-winning exhibits: Jaguar Cove, Trail of Vines, Northern Trail, Tropical Rain Forest, Elephant Forest, and African Savanna. It's a very family-

friendly place with well-marked paths, concessions facilities, fun facts, and extremely knowledgeable staff. Toddlers will love Zoomazium, an indoor play space that also offers programs such as storytelling, puppet shows, and music and body movement.

Museums

Children's Museum
Center House, Seattle Center, 305 Harrison Street; tel: 206-441-1768; www.thechildrens museum.org; Mon–Fri 10am–5pm, Sat–Sun 10am–6pm; admission charge; bus: 1, 2, 8,

monorail; map p.130 B2
For toddlers and young children this museum is a dream come true, with lots of hands-on activities from

Wondering what to do with older kids and teens? Take them up the **Space Needle** to see the lay of the land, on **Bill Speidel's Underground Tour** to learn the low-down of Seattle's bawdy early days, or to the **Experience Music Project** to rub shoulders with rock stars. *See also Architecture, p.26–7; Museums and Galleries, p.76–8.*

Left and below left: kids run wild at the wonderful Woodland Park Zoo.

kids and adults alike, from dinosaurs to robots to virtual technology. The Science Playground demystifies the wonders of science, and in the Saltwater Tidal Pool you can gently touch sea creatures and watch the tides working. There is also a tropical Butterfly House with free-flying butterflies and a chrysalis-viewing window. The Planetarium is the place to learn about the stars and the planets. There's also a laser dome theater (schedule tel: 206-443-2850) and two IMAX theaters (tel: 206-443-4629).

Tours

Ride the Ducks

516 Broad Street, Seattle Center; tel: 206-441-3825; www.ridethe ducksofseattle.com; admission charge; daily 10am–6pm every half hour; bus: 3, 4, 74; map p.130 B2

This company provides fun, 90-minute guided tours of the city's roadways and waterways on open-air World War II amphibious vehicles. The lively commentary and adventurous journey is sure to captivate young imaginations.

painting in the Imagination Studio (smocks provided) and watching small balls move through tubes at Cog City to dressing up in Global Village. It's a terrific kid-sized museum.

Odyssey Maritime Discovery Center

2205 Alaskan Way, Pier 66, Downtown; tel: 206-374-4000; www.ody.org; Tue–Thur 10am–3pm, Fri 10am–4pm, Sat–Sun 11am–5pm; admission charge; bus: 99; map p.132 B3

Another hands-on museum, also good for older kids, where you learn about the region's maritime history while loading and unloading a model container ship, going on a virtual kayak through the San Juan Islands, or using pedal power to get a propeller to spin.

Pacific Science Center

200 2nd Avenue N, Seattle Center; tel: 206-443-2001; www.pacsci.org; Mon–Fri 10am–5pm, Sat–Sun 10am–6pm; admission charge; bus: 1, 2, 8, monorail; map

The city's public parks provide a great place for kids to let off steam. Many have well-equipped playgrounds (Green Lake, Volunteer Park), swimming areas (Green Lake, Seward Park), and wonderful beaches for playing in the sand (Alki, Golden Gardens). Bring a picnic and enjoy a free family outing. *See also Parks, Gardens, and Beaches, p.94–9.*

p.130 A2

This vibrant, educational, and fun science museum has tons of exhibits that will engage

Right: kids of all ages will enjoy the Ride the Ducks tour.

Coffee Shops

Caffeine flows through the veins of most Seattleites, and this is hardly surprising given that the world's best-known coffee shop, Starbucks, originated here, as did its much smaller rival Tully's. But the true experience is to be found in the quirky, independently owned coffee shops dotted around Seattle that serve as gathering places for home workers, students, retired folks, moms and tots, and just about everyone else. Most offer WiFi, some present author readings, lectures, or concerts, but all serve up good-quality coffee. For good measure, the occasional teashop is included.

Downtown and Belltown

Caffe Migliore
1215 4th Avenue; tel: 206-624-9893; www.caffemigliore.com; Mon–Fri 6am–5.30pm; bus: 24, 33; map p.133 D2
In the heart of the financial district, this elegant café serves traditional Italian coffees in a tranquil setting. It tends to draw a well-heeled clientele, with a sophisticated atmosphere. The baristas know their stuff.

Caffe Senso Unico
622 Olive Way; tel: 206-264-7611; Mon–Fri 6am–5pm, Sat 7.30am–4pm; bus: 25, 66, 70;

> It's not uncommon to be in a completely packed coffee shop, with every possible seat taken, yet it's as quiet as a church with all the patrons plugged into their laptops, headphones, and tapping away on their keyboards.

map p.133 D3
An authentic Italian café, sophisticated, upscale, and serving some of the best cappuccino in town. The Italian owner runs a tight ship, and the drinks are served in attractive cups and mugs,

with pastries to tempt you. You can leaf through Italian travel magazines, or admire the art on the walls.

Dilettante Mocha Café
400 Pine Street, in Westlake Center; tel: 206-903-8595; www.dilettante.com; Mon–Sat 10am–9pm, Sun 11am–6pm; bus: 10, 43, 49; map p.133 D3
Take a break from shopping in this rather elegant café on the main floor of Westlake Center (see p.117). Dilettante is known for its chocolates, and in addition to the wide range of hot chocolates and mochas, there are tempting

Left: drinkers at Victrola Coffee (*see p.40*) take advantage of the WiFi connection.

umbria.com; Mon–Fri 6am–6pm, Sat 7am–6pm, Sun 8am–5pm; bus: 15, 18, 28; map p.134 B3

Upscale Italian café with traditional espresso drinks, wine, beer, light lunches, pastries, and *gelato*. It serves its own roasts, skillfully blended for different tastes. Its sophisticated space, in one of Pioneer Square's old red-brick buildings, is light and airy.

Elliott Bay Café
101 S. Main Street; tel: 206-682-6664; www.elliottbay book.com; Mon–Sat 8am–8pm, Sun 10am–6pm; bus: 15, 18, 21; map p.134 B3

In the basement of this fantastic independent bookstore is a large bohemian café serving coffees, teas, and substantial sandwiches and soups made from organic ingredients. Mixing scholastic and hippy influences, it's a good meeting point in Pioneer Square. The place is jam-packed during author events.

Zeitgeist
171 S. Jackson Street; tel: 206-583-0497; www.zeitgeistcoffee. com; Mon–Fri 6am–7pm,

With their late hours, lots of coffee shops are a mellow alternative to bars for a good social scene, with decent music and some providing board games (scrabble, chess, and such).

truffles and decadent cakes for you to try.

Top Pot
2124 5th Avenue; tel: 206-728-1966; www.toppotdoughnuts. com; Mon–Fri 6am–7pm, Sat–Sun 7am–7pm; bus: 1, 2, 13; map p.133 C4

Awesome hand-forged doughnuts, strong coffee, herbal teas, and a bookish atmosphere set Top Pot aside from many competitors. The retro atmosphere is a nice change, and the doughnuts transport you back to childhood.
(Also on Capitol Hill, p.39.)

Uptown Espresso
2504 4th Avenue; tel: 206-441-1084; www.uptownespresso.net; Mon–Thur 5am–10pm, Fri 5am–11pm, Sat 6am–11pm,

Sun 6am–10pm; bus: 1, 2, 13; map p.132 B4

This large Belltown branch of Uptown Espresso, self-proclaimed 'home of the velvet foam,' is perfect for settling in for a few hours. There are comfy armchairs in the windows, and outdoor seating, too.
(Also at: 4301 SW Edmunds Street, West Seattle; tel: 206-935-3753.)

Pioneer Square and the International District
Caffe Umbria
320 Occidental Avenue S; tel: 206-624-5847; www.caffe

Left: try a Top Pot doughnut with your coffee. **Right:** friendly Uptown Espresso.

Sat–Sun 8am–7pm; bus: 15, 18, 28; map p.134 B3

With its brick walls and art-work that changes regularly, this warm and inviting coffee shop has a strong connection to the Seattle arts scene, as evidenced by the crowds that converge here on the 1st Thursday art walk route *(see p.80)*.

Seattle Center and Lower Queen Anne

Caffe Ladro
600 Queen Anne Avenue N; tel: 206-282-1549; www.caffe ladro.com; daily 5.30am–11pm; bus: 1, 8, 15; map p.130 A3

Serving only fair-trade, organic, shade-grown coffee, Caffe Ladro sets the bar high. Its delicious baked goods include savory quiches, pastries, muffins, and a range of yummy desserts.

(Also at : 425 N. 36th St, Fremont, tel: 206-675-0854; 7001 California Avenue SW, West Seattle, tel: 206-938-8021.)

Uptown Espresso
525 Queen Anne Avenue N; tel: 206-285-3757; www.uptownespresso.net; Mon–Thur 5am–10pm, Fri 5am–11pm, Sat 6am–11pm, Sun 6am–10pm; bus: 1, 8, 15; map p.130 A3

The most charming branch of this small chain of coffee shops, mismatched and antique furniture and a warm atmosphere greet you here. Service can be erratic, but it's such a pleasant place to be that it doesn't matter much.

Capitol Hill

Bauhaus Books & Coffee
301 E. Pine Street; tel: 206-625-1600; Mon–Fri 6am–1am, Sun 8am–1am; bus: 14, 43, 49

Good for people-watching, especially from the sidewalk chairs. Inside, it's a little crowded and hard to have a conversation without your neighbors being involved,

and the music can be overwhelming, but the fact that it's been around for years attests to its enduring popularity.

Caffé Vita
1005 E. Pike Street; tel: 206-709-4440; www.caffevita.com; Mon–Fri 6am–11pm, Sat–Sun 7am–11pm; bus: 10, 12

This heavy-hitter among coffee shops serves up strong, delicious coffee. The dark, subdued décor is good for chilling out and taking a break from the lively streets of Capitol Hill.

Joe Bar
810 E. Roy Street; tel: 206-324-0407; www.joebar.org; Mon–Fri 7.30am–9.30pm, Sat–Sun 8.30am–9.30pm; bus: 9, 49

This tiny hole-in-the-wall is a cozy hangout for students from neighboring Cornish College, and they serve delicious crepes and paninis. Besides coffees and teas, wine and beer are also served here. The tiny second-story balconies, reached by steep, narrow staircases, make you feel like you're in a doll's house.

Left: coffee and computers at Online Coffee Company. **Right:** cozy Joe Bar on Capitol Hill.

Left: Bauhaus Books & Coffee.

Online Coffee Company
1404 E. Pine Street; tel: 206-323-7798; www.onlinecoffee co.com; daily 7am–10pm; bus: 8, 43

One of a few Internet cafés in town, here you can use one of a dozen or more computer terminals (half-hour free with cup of coffee/tea), or bring your laptop. There are also a few sofas for lounging. They serve the usual espresso drinks, plus beer. Patio seats in front.

Remedy Teas
345 15th Avenue E; tel: 206-323-4TEA; www.remedyteas.com; daily 7am–11pm; bus: 8, 10, 43

With over 150 varieties of loose-leaf teas, and special organic blends geared towards deep sleep, digestive ailments, or hangover cures, this tranquil modern teashop fills a much-needed gap in a city that's highly wired. Lovely outdoor patio, calm, cool interior, and open late daily – the perfect way to unwind after a long day.

Top Pot
609 Summit Avenue E; tel: 206-323-7841; www.toppotdough nuts.com; Mon–Fri 6am–9pm, Sat–Sun 7am–9pm; bus: 14

One of the best neighborhood coffee shops, hands down. Avoid weekend mornings, when the line of people in need of coffee and scrumptious doughnuts reaches out the door and there's nowhere to sit. But other times it's relaxed, mellow, and with pleasant

Loyalty cards are available from a lot of coffee shops, so you might purchase 10 drinks and get your 11th free. Some also offer store cards, which you can load up with $20 or $30, for instance, and just swipe each time you come in.

Left: Victrola Coffee has free newspapers and a friendly vibe.

coffee.com; daily 5.30am–11pm; bus: 8, 10, 43
The original Victrola on 15th is one of the true coffee hangouts, with a great vibe, talented baristas, and lots of tables and chairs for settling in with your laptop, newspaper, or chatting with friends. The random collection of sidewalk chairs makes for good people-watching.

Fremont

Fremont Coffee Company
459 N 36th Street; tel: 206-623-3633; www.fremontcoffee.net; Mon–Fri 6am–9pm, Sat 7am–9pm, Sun 7am–8pm; bus: 28, 46
A community-minded coffee shop, this eco-friendly establishment has solar panels that run the dishwasher and heat the downstairs. It's located in a charming 1904 house with original features and a sizeable deck. Have a strong coffee or home-brewed root beer accompanied by house-made quiches with herbs from the garden, paninis, and other baked goods. Beer and mimosas are also available.

Simply Desserts
3421 Fremont Avenue N; tel: 206-633-2671; www.simplydesserts.com; Tue and Thur noon–10pm, Fri–Sat noon–11.30pm, Sun noon–6pm; bus: 26, 28, 31
This is the place in Fremont for coffee and late-night desserts, or something to tempt your sweet tooth any time of the day. A tiny hole-in-the-wall with just a few tables, it serves up mouthwateringly decadent cakes, tortes, and cheesecakes.

Ballard

Café Besalu
5909 24th Avenue; tel: 206-789-1463; Wed–Sun 7am–3pm; bus: 18

outdoor seating too.
(Also in Belltown, *see p.37*)

Victrola Cafe and Roastery
310 E. Pike Street; tel: 206-624-1725; www.victrolacoffee.com; Mon–Fri 6.30am–8pm, Sat–Sun 7.30am–8pm; bus: 11, 14, 49
Flooded with light from its floor-to-ceiling windows, this airy venue with rough brick walls, polished concrete floor and solid wood tables is a sophisticated spot for a coffee (also serves beer, wine, and small range of snacks). Free cuppings (coffee-tastings) Wednesdays at 11am.

Victrola Coffee & Art
411 15th Avenue E; tel: 206-325-6520; www.victrola

A lot of coffee shops have community bulletin boards where there are notices for everything from accommodations to pet-walking to furniture-building. They also stock the free newspapers, such as *Seattle Weekly*, *The Stranger*, and local community papers.

One of the nicest things is that you never feel rushed in Seattle's coffee shops. They are designed for hanging out, and lots of people settle in with a book or the newspaper or friends for hours on end.

Besalu's Viennese-trained baker and proprietor makes some of the best European-style pastries in town at this Ballard favorite. Crowds line up for the quiche that comes hot out of the oven at 10am. Local roaster Lighthouse coffee is used to turn out good cappuccinos and lattes.

Floating Leaves Tea
2213 NW Market Street; tel: 206-529-4268; www.floating leaves.com; Mon and Wed–Sat 11am–10pm, Sun noon–8pm; bus: 44, 46

Zen-like teashop whose friendly owners travel to the mountains of Taiwan and to Japan to source the best leaves. White tea, green tea, oolong, black tea, and puer (fermented) tea are all offered, with instruction in steeping the leaves (between 5 and 15 times), and in sipping the tea, and smelling the incredible aroma through fragrance cups.

Miro Tea
5405 Ballard Avenue NW; tel: 206-782-6832;

www.mirotea.com; Mon–Sat 8am–10pm, Sun 8am–8pm; bus: 17, 44, 46

Step inside this retro tea-shop and it feels like you've walked into a 1960s living room. Mellow, comfortable, with a great selection of teas (though on the pricey side) and crepes. Work on your laptop, or play a game of scrabble with a friend.

Vérité Coffee and Cupcake Royale
2052 NW Market Street; tel: 206-782-9557; www.verite coffee.com; Mon–Fri 6.30am–10pm, Sat 6.30am–11pm, Sun 7.30am–9pm; bus: 44, 46

With a tantalizing selection of frosting-swirled cupcakes and Stumptown coffee, Vérité is a magnet for kids, hipsters, and grandmas alike. Go for the perennial favorite, 'Holly Hobby' – a vanilla buttercream cupcake finished off with rainbow sprinkles. This is one of the heavy-hitters in Seattle, with well-trained baristas serving up flavorful coffee.
(Also at 4556 California Avenue SW, West Seattle, tel: 206-932-2971.)

West Seattle
Alki Bakery
2738 Alki Avenue W; tel: 206-935-1352; www.alkibakery.com; daily 8am–8.30pm; bus: 37, 53

This beachfront bakery serves up soups and sandwiches as well as delicious pies and espresso. Great for people-watching and enjoying the views of Puget Sound. They also serve a good breakfast, and offer heartier fare for dinner.

Bakery Nouveau
4737 California Avenue SW; tel: 206-923-0534; www.bakery

nouveau.com; Mon–Thur 6am–7pm, Fri 6am–10pm, Sat 7am–10pm, Sun 7.30am–7pm; bus: 22, 54, 85

Enjoy a fabulous array of flaky French pastries, rich cakes, or savory delights (including quiches and filled baguettes) with your coffee. The twice-baked almond croissants are a big hit, but get there early or they'll be gone.

C&P Coffee Company
5612 California Avenue SW; tel: 206-933-3125; www.candp coffee.com; Mon–Fri 6.30am–8pm, Sat–Sun 7am–8pm; bus: 22, 54 85

Lighthouse Roasters coffee and a range of loose-leaf teas are served in this lovely coffee shop, located in a comfy 1907 craftsman-style house in West Seattle. It also hosts regular live music events.

Coffee to a Tea
5451 California Avenue SW; tel: 206-937-1495; www.sugar rushbakingcompany.com; Mon–Thur and Sat 8am–8pm, Fri 8am–10pm, Sun 8am–6pm; bus: 22, 55, 85

Devoted customers come back again and again for the gorgeous and delicious little cupcakes, arguably the best in Seattle. The long, thin café has a kids' play area at the back, and a little patio in the front.

Left: enjoy a brew at Miro Tea.
Right: Coffee to a Tea's delicious handmade cupcakes.

Environment

In 2005 Seattle Mayor Greg Nickels launched the US Mayors Climate Protection Agreement designed to meet the goals of the Kyoto Protocol (the international agreement to address global warming that was ratified by over 140 countries, but notably not by the United States). Mayor Nickels and more than 400 other US mayors who signed up to the agreement have pledged to reduce greenhouse gas emissions in their own communities. Visitors to Seattle can contribute to the city's green goals by using public transportation, eating locally sourced food, and carrying refillable water bottles.

Stewardship of the Environment

The health of the region's rivers, lakes, and Puget Sound are vital to the survival of marine mammals and fish. Stopping heavy industry's seepage of toxins (especially harmful mercury and PCBs) into the environment is a priority, as is cleaning up existing contaminants that are damaging wildlife. Alongside this are efforts to restore wetlands and shorelines. A couple of small but successful examples are the wetlands at **Golden Gardens** and the beach at the **Olympic Sculpture Park**.

In order to reduce household waste that ends up in landfills, the city provides curbside collection of glass, paper, plastic, cans, and also food and yard waste, which

is turned into compost. The Mayor's office is encouraging residents to drink the mountain-fed tap water in preference to bottled water, and to bring their own reusable shopping bags to the grocery store. The city council recently passed a law that will levy a 20-cent charge per plastic or paper bag at supermarkets and drugstores. The law goes into effect in January 2009.
SEE ALSO PARKS, GARDENS, AND BEACHES, P.95–6, 97

Greener Transportation

Ongoing population growth in the Puget Sound region is putting additional strain on

an already congested road network. This, combined with the high prices of fuel, has encouraged some Seattleites to opt for greener forms of transportation, such as carpooling, to take advantage of the **HOV (High-Occupancy Vehicle) lanes** on freeways, which flow much faster than standard lanes during rush hour.

Use of **Metro Transit's** fleet of part-hybrid diesel and electric-powered buses is also up. To encourage drivers to leave their cars at home, Downtown is a designated ride-free zone, which means that you can hop on and off the buses without having to

> The giant cruise ships that dock along Seattle's waterfront, some of them accommodating thousands of passengers, now plug into electric shore power instead of running their engines, thus considerably reducing pollution.

Left: the South Lake Union Streetcar runs on electricity.

Seattle City Light, the publicly owned electric utility, uses renewable energy sources and carbon offsets to achieve net-zero greenhouse gas emissions, and was the first public utility in the nation to do so.

smaller efforts, such as the **Fremont Coffee Company** with its solar panels.
SEE ALSO COFFEE SHOPS, P.40; OUTDOOR ACTIVITIES, P.91

Sustainable Food

At weekly farmers' markets fresh produce direct from the farm is available, empowering community-supported agriculture and ensuring a smaller carbon footprint. The city also has a number of supermarkets that stock a wide range of organic, fair-trade, and locally sourced foods; among these are **PCC Natural Market**, **Whole Foods**, and **Madison Market Co-op**.
SEE ALSO FOOD AND DRINK, P.57

Left: the shipping industry is a major pollutant.

pay a fare. And in 2007 the electric-powered **South Lake Union Streetcar** was inaugurated, with service between Westlake Center and Eastlake, through the rapidly redeveloping South Lake Union neighborhood.

Sound Transit's light rail link from Sea-Tac International Airport to Downtown via Columbia City and the Rainier Valley in South Seattle opens in 2009, with an extension north to the University District via Capitol Hill due to be completed in 2016.

For those who don't need to drive regularly but aren't yet ready to give up the car, **Zip Cars** operates a car-share scheme that eliminates the expense of owning, maintaining, and insuring a private vehicle, yet still offers the convenience of having access to a car when you need one.
SEE ALSO TRANSPORTATION, P.126–7

Right: two wheels are better than four at REI's 'green' flagship store.

Eco-friendly Construction

Architects and developers are embracing green construction to reduce buildings' energy consumption while employing sustainable materials. A few examples are the **Ballard Public Library**, which has a living roof, **REI**'s flagship store, **City Hall**, and **King Street Station**. There are also many

Essentials

Be sure to take a few moments to equip yourself with essential information on communication, health care, money, and tourist information before you travel, so you will be free to enjoy your visit once you arrive. Seattle has good emergency services and medical care, but it's vital that you have adequate health insurance since medical care can be very expensive. To stay in touch with the folks back home, many hotels, coffee shops, Internet cafés and the public libraries offer Internet access. The Seattle Convention and Visitors Bureau, and Washington State Tourism are useful resources for more information.

Crime and Safety

The streets of Seattle are relatively safe during the day. At night, avoid walking alone on deserted streets. Exercise common sense by always locking your car (leaving no valuables in sight), use your hotel's safety deposit box to store your valuables, and carry only the cash you need. If you are the victim of theft, report it to the local police department.
Seattle Police Department
Non-emergency tel: 206-625-5011
Emergencies: 911

Embassies and Consulates

Australia
401 Andover Park E, Seattle, WA 98188; tel: 206-575-7446
Canada
1501 4th Avenue, Suite 600, Seattle, WA 98101; tel: 206-443-1777
Ireland
2234 Massachusetts Avenue NW, Washington, DC 20008; tel: 202-462-3939
New Zealand
37 Observatory Circle NW,
Washington, D.C. 20008; tel: 202-328-4800
United Kingdom
1 Sansome Street, Suite 850, San Francisco, CA 94104; tel: 415-617-1300

Internet Access

Most Seattle hotels, libraries, and coffee shops offer wired (and often WiFi) Internet connection. There are also a few Internet cafés, and all branches of the Seattle Public Library allow visitors to use computers for a limited time.
Cyber-Dogs
909 Pike Street; www.cyber-dogs.com
Online Coffee Company
1720 E. Olive Way; www.onlinecoffeeco.com
Seattle Central Library
1000 4th Avenue; www.spl.org

Medical Care

HEALTH INSURANCE
Medical care can be prohibitively expensive if you are uninsured; it is essential that you obtain adequate health insurance before traveling to the US.

HOSPITALS
Children's Hospital and Medical Center
4800 Sand Point Way NE; tel: 206-987-2000
Harborview Medical Center
325 9th Avenue; tel: 206-731-3000
Swedish Medical Center
747 Broadway; tel: 206-386-6000

Western Washington enjoys a mild climate, with average daytime temperatures ranging from a pleasant 75–79°F (23–26°C) in summer and 41–48°F (4.5–9°C) in winter. Most of the city's legendary rain (37.7ins/957.6mm a year, on average) falls from October through April. Seattleites are used to this, and often brave the elements without an umbrella. The mountains receive abundant snow, making great conditions for skiers but hazards for drivers. The higher hills and outlying areas also receive snow from time to time, but Seattle rarely receives much. Late spring through early fall are the driest and warmest times to visit.

Left: checking emails at the Online Coffee Company.

Postal Services and Telephones

POST OFFICES
There are branches of the post office throughout Seattle, but the main branch is located Downtown at 301 Union Street. Most operate Monday to Friday from 9.30am–5.30pm.

TELEPHONES
Greater Seattle area codes are 206 (Seattle), 425 (East-side), and 253 (South End). To dial long-distance within the US or Canada first dial 1. International calls require 011 + (country code) + (city code) + (number). Country codes: Australia 61, Ireland 353, New Zealand 64, South Africa 27, UK 44.

Tourist Information

Seattle's Convention and Visitors Bureau
1 Convention Place, 701 Pike Street; tel. 206-461-5840; www.visitseattle.org/visitors; Mon–Fri 8.30am–5pm (summer: daily 9am–5pm).
Washington State Tourism
www.experiencewashington.com

Visas and Passports

To enter the US you need a valid passport. Check with the US embassy in your home country to see if you also require a visa. For more information, visit http://travel.state.gov

---

Disabled travelers can obtain information about discounts, transportation, assistive technology, community resources, and more from the City of Seattle's Human Services website (www.seattle.gov/human services/aging/disability.htm) or by calling 206-386-1001.

Money

ATMS
ATMs (cash machines) are readily found at banks, grocery stores, and in many public places.

CURRENCY AND CREDIT CARDS
Foreign currency exchange is available at Sea-Tac International Airport, major banks, and large Downtown hotels. Credit and debit cards are widely accepted.
For lost or stolen cards, call: 1-800-336-8472 for Visa; 1-800-826-2181 for MasterCard.

TAX AND TIPPING
Washington state sales tax is currently 8.9 percent, with additional tax for hotels and restaurants (varies by

county). The accepted rates for tips are 15–20 percent of the pre-tax bill for waiting staff (10 percent for bar staff) and 10–15 percent for taxi drivers.

TRAVELER'S CHECKS
American dollar traveler's checks are acceptable as cash in many stores, restaurants, and hotels. Bring your passport for ID when you cash them.
To report stolen or lost traveler's checks call:
American Express
tel: 1-800-221-7282
MasterCard
tel: 1-800-223-9920
Thomas Cook
tel: 1-800-223-7373
Visa
tel: 1-800-227-6811

Excursions

Jagged mountain peaks, Victorian towns, quiet islands, and a temperate rainforest are all within reach of Seattle. The jewels of Puget Sound are the San Juan Islands, the archipelago that gets more sunshine than the surrounding area. The Sound is known for its wildlife, including orcas, bald eagles, and bears. The ski slopes and hiking trails of the Cascades, the glacial Mt Rainier and Mt St Helens, plus many islands with beaches, fishing, and water sports, all mean there's plenty to enjoy outside Seattle for either a day out, or a trip for a week or more. For a selection of places to stay outside the city, *see Hotels, p.71–3.*

Islands

WHIDBEY ISLAND

Whidbey Island is the longest contiguous island in the US. Ferries from Mukilteo (45 minutes north of Seattle) or Port Townsend (on the Olympic Peninsula) transport you to its rolling hills and rocky beaches. The town of **Langley** perches on a cliff over Saratoga Passage, with water and mountain views a backdrop to the century-old shops, restaurants, art galleries, and inns. **Coupeville** has Victorian homes and shops, and **Oak Harbor** is the largest town, with Whidbey Naval Air Station nearby. At the northern tip of the island, narrow **Deception Pass** is spanned by a 180-ft (55-m) high steel bridge to Fidalgo Island, while attractive, 19th-century **Anacortes** is the ferry terminal for the San Juan Islands and Vancouver Island.

SAN JUAN ISLANDS

Of the many San Juan Islands, only four – Shaw, Lopez, Orcas, and San Juan – have regular ferry service;

the others can be reached by floatplane or chartered sailboat, via narrow channels and open water, passing on the way sandy beaches, shallow bays, sand spits, grassy estuaries, and forested slopes. Orcas (killer whales), seabirds, harbor seals, otters, and bald eagles can be spotted on this leisurely route. The flat rural terrain of **Lopez**, **Shaw**, and **San Juan** are great for bicycling.

Orcas Island was named not for the whales but for the Spanish patron of an explorer of the region in 1792. Bed-and-breakfast inns are all over the island, but the only

Left: sunset over Lopez island.

traditional resort is **Rosario** (tel: 866-801-ROCK/7625; www.rosarioresort.com), the handsome 1904 estate of shipbuilder and former Seattle mayor Robert Moran, for whom **Moran State Park** is named. A paved road and hiking trail winds up Mt Constitution to a 50ft (15m) high stone lookout tower.

On **San Juan Island**, the ferry docks at **Friday Harbor**, a highly attractive village of restaurants, hotels, and shops. The **Whale Museum** (tel: 360-378-4710; www.whale-museum.org) explains whale behavior and sounds and displays photos of the region's resident orcas, whose distinctive markings

Check out the websites for the National Parks before you travel. They have good maps for hiking, up-to-date information on road closures, and list the campsites and other accommodation options with their fees. You can also find out whether a permit is needed.

Left: Mt Rainier towers over the Olympic Peninsula.

com/empress). Opened in 1908, its elegant French chateau-style architecture and manicured grounds set the tone for a refined visit, and what better way to start than with afternoon high tea. The other grand buildings facing the harbor are the **British Columbia Government Parliament Buildings** (tours tel: 250-387-3046), designed in 1898 by 25-year-old English architect Francis Rattenbury, who made a fortune in British Columbia's Gold Rush. An imposing mix of European styles, Parliament is especially impressive at night when illuminated by thousands of light bulbs. Other must-sees include the outstanding **Royal British Columbia Museum** (tel: 250-356-7226; www.royalbcmuseum.bc.ca) and the world-famous **Butchart Gardens** (tel: 250-652-4422; www.butchartgardens.com), outside the town.

SEE ALSO TRANSPORTATION, P.127

Cascade Mountains

MT RAINIER

On a clear day, the spectacular snow-covered Mt Rainier is an awesome sight. The fifth-highest summit in

---

> Distances can be deceptive, and it can take a lot longer to get to and through some of the National Parks than you might think. Fill up the gas tank when you have the opportunity to do so, bring snacks and beverages, and take breaks before you get too tired.

---

enable researchers to follow individuals in each 'pod'; in 2006, Puget Sound was designated a critical habitat for orcas. Relics of a dispute between Great Britain and the US between 1859–72 can be found in the **San Juan Island National Historical Park**. Charming **Roche Harbor**, once the richest deposit of limestone west of the Mississippi, is at the island's north end. At the harbor's edge is the delightful 1880s Hotel de Haro (tel: 800-451-8910; www.rocheharbor.com).

VICTORIA, BRITISH COLUMBIA

Located on the southern end of Vancouver Island, in Canadian coastal waters, Victoria is an enticing and easy getaway by seaplane with Kenmore Air or on the Victoria Clipper from Pier 69. A valid passport is required to enter Canada (Washington state residents can use an enhanced driver's license).

Victoria, the capital of British Columbia, is known for its quaint English character, with double-decker buses, well-tended gardens, and high tea. The center of Victoria is the Inner Harbor. Facing it is the grand, ivy-clad **Empress Hotel** (tel: 250-384-8111; www.fairmont.

Right: the harbor at Victoria.

the contiguous United States, it soars to 14,408ft (4,392m). A single road loops the mountain, through much of the 378-sq-mile (980-sq-km) **Mt Rainier National Park** (www.nps.gov/mora). The park is open all year, but in winter the Cayuse and Chinook passes are closed.

At **Longmire**, just inside the southwestern border near the **Nisqually entrance**, the modestly priced National Park Inn (tel: 360-569-2275) is the only lodge open all year; the rustic inn also has a wildlife museum. Longmire is also the only place in the park to buy gas. **Paradise** is the most popular destination, with the Henry M. Jackson Memorial Visitors' Center, a gift shop, and a cafeteria. There are spectacular views of Narada Falls and Nisqually Glacier, as well as of the

Nature-lovers and bird-spotters will marvel at the abundance of nature in western Washington. Bald eagles, deer, moose, and orca whales are among the wildlife you may be lucky to see.

mountain itself. Accommodation is available at the fabulous Paradise Inn (tel: 360-569-2275), built in 1917.

Head east, then north at the **Stevens Canyon entrance** in the park's southeast corner, to the 4,675-ft (1,425-m) Cayuse Pass. Just beyond the pass is the **White River entrance**. Turn left to stop by the **Sunrise Visitors' Center** (at 6,400ft/1,950m), a breathtaking entry to lush wild-flower meadows. The Emmons Glacier, largest in the lower 48 states, is visible from a trail by the visitors' center.

North of the White River entrance is **Crystal Mountain**, with some of the best winter skiing and snowboarding in the state of Washington. In summer, you can swap your skis for hiking boots or take advantage of horseback riding.

MT ST HELENS
On May 18, 1980 this snow-covered mountain erupted with such violence that it blew 1,314ft (400m) off its top, sending a massive plume of ash into the atmosphere,

causing devastating mudslides, and taking the lives of 57 people and millions of animals and fish. In the decades since, the trees and plants have grown again, and the wildlife has returned, but geologists carefully monitor the volcano for further activity. The area is now designated as the **Mt St Helens National Volcanic Monument** (tel: 360-449 7800; www.fs.fed.us/gpnf/mshnvm). Five visitors' centers dot the Spirit Lake highway, all supplying information on the eruption.

NORTH CASCADES HIGHWAY
State Route 20 is a spectacularly scenic highway that winds through the **North Cascades National Park** (www.nps.gov/noca), traversing jagged snow-covered mountains, rushing rivers, and high waterfalls. The park has a large concentration of glaciers that end in ice-blue lakes, with meadows blan-

Right: tulips laid out for the Skagit Valley Tulip Festival, and Skagit Valley bathed in morning mist.

Left: a snowy North Cascades National Park.

...keting small corners between broken rock spires.

LEAVENWORTH

Some 135 miles (217km) east of Seattle, across the Cascade Mountains, lies this surprising gem of a town. In a bid to revive the flagging economy when the logging industry died down in the 1960s, Leavenworth (www.leavenworth. org) was re-branded as a Bavarian village, and is now complete with Alpine architecture, German food and music, and even a **Nutcracker Museum** (tel: 800-892-2389; www.nutcrackermuseum.com).

If you're planning to travel by ferry to the Olympic Peninsula or one of the Islands, check the schedule (www.wsdot.wa/gov/ ferries) and arrive at the terminal in plenty of time. Friday and Sunday afternoons are the busiest times to travel, and if you're not there very early you could have a very long wait.

During winter it is blanketed in snow, and over the holidays the town's buildings are beautifully decorated with lights, while Christmas carols fill the air. The area has great opportunities for snowshoeing and cross-country skiing, and in summer there's good hiking and horseback riding.

North Sound

SKAGIT VALLEY

Heading north on I 5 from Seattle, you'll come to the attractive Skagit Valley, a farming community famous for its tulips. Visitors in busloads come each April to attend the Skagit Valley Tulip Festival, when farmers open up their fields to the public. The small town of **Mt Vernon**, with its historic red-brick buildings, is a good place to start, since this is where the festival office is located, but the cute town of **La Conner** offers more amenities for tourists, being filled with art galleries, antique stores, restaurants, and charming bed & breakfasts.

BELLINGHAM

The roadway curves north about 25 miles (40km) and follows the water up to Bellingham, a bustling university town (home to Western Wash-

Left: Victorian buildings in Port Townsend.

ington University), where a good number of top-notch restaurants serve regional oysters and seafood. Adjacent to Bellingham is the attractive town of **Fairhaven**, with its antiques stores, bistros, and boutiques. A more scenic route to take up to Bellingham is **Chuckanut Drive** (Route 11), a historic part of the old Pacific Highway that goes through the Skagit Valley and north along the coast. It's one of the state's most scenic drives, and a pleasant alternative to I 5.

Olympic Peninsula

PORT TOWNSEND

Once a booming port town, Port Townsend is today a popular destination for a weekend getaway, with its well-preserved Victorian buildings containing art galleries, hotels, and excellent restaurants. The Visitor Center (tel: 360-385-2722; www.enjoypt.com) has maps and information.

North of town are the 434 acres (175 hectares) of historic **Fort Worden**, keystone of an 1880s network of forts, which guarded the entrance

to Puget Sound until the end of World War II. The fort is now a state park. Sharing the flat point with gun emplacements is the **Point Wilson Lighthouse**, built in 1922.

OLYMPIC NATIONAL PARK

A UNESCO biosphere reserve and World Heritage Site, this spectacular park offers abundant nature to explore. The Olympic National Park Visitor Center (tel: 360-565 3130; www.nps.gov/olym) in **Port Angeles** has maps and park information, and displays on the wildlife, plants, geology, and the tribal culture of the Northwest Coast. To enter the park, follow Race Street in Port Angeles to the well-marked Hurricane Ridge Road, and then make the steep 17-mile (27km) ascent through dense forest to reach **Hurricane Ridge**, 5,200ft

Right: Point Wilson Lighthouse.

(1,600m) above sea level. From here are views of mountains, Alpine meadows with wild flowers, and forests as well as nature trails.

To the southwest is glacier-capped **Mount Olympus**, at 7,965ft (2,428m) the highest peak in the Olympics. No roads lead to Mount Olympus, only hiking trails. Beyond Port Angeles, Highway 101 curves south around **Lake Crescent**, an immense cobalt-blue glacially carved lake surrounded by tall-timbered forest. Gorgeous Lake Crescent Lodge (tel: 360-928 3211), on the southern shore, is where President Franklin D. Roosevelt stayed in 1937 before he signed the act creating the 922,000-acre (373,000-hectare) Olympic National Park.

The **Hoh Rainforest Visitor Center** (tel: 360-374 6925) is south of Forks off US 101 and about 20 miles (30km) into the park. There is a wealth of information here on the wildlife, flora, and the history of the temperate rainforest. Moisture-laden air from the Pacific drenches the area

with more than 150ins (380cm) of rain annually – this is the wettest place in the lower 48 states. Three loop trails lead into the rainforest of moss-draped trees, ferns, and a clear, glacial-fed river. Moose, deer, and other animals are often seen.

Farther south of the turnoff, US 101 swings west to the coast and follows cliffs overlooking beautiful beaches, from **Ruby Beach** and the **Hoh Indian Reservation** in the north to driftwood-covered **Kalaloch Beach** in the south. Part of Olympic National Park's coastal strip, the coast has a rugged and picturesque beauty. Waves crash against rocks and off-shore islands, casting tree trunks up on the shore like toothpicks. A few miles offshore is reef-girdled **Destruc-**

Left: moss-draped Hoh Rainforest, and an Olympic National Park beach at sunset.

tion Island and its lighthouse, built in 1890. On a foggy day, the mournful foghorn disturbs thousands of auklets – small seabirds – on the island. The forest surrounding Lake Quinault is often called 'the other rainforest.' It's possible to drive a 25-mile (40km) loop around the glacial lake. **Lake Quinault Lodge** (tel: 360-288 2900), a huge, old-fashioned cedar hotel built in 1926 on the lake's southern shore, is a landmark. Winding trails lead from the lodge into the rainforest.

If you're planning to drive into the mountains during late fall, winter, or early spring, check the road conditions to see if chains are required. Conditions can change rapidly, so it's a good idea to have chains just in case. It's also a good idea to pack blankets, food, and beverages in case of road closures or other delays.

Festivals

Hundreds of festivals punctuate the calendar throughout the Puget Sound region. The Seattle Center hosts some of the biggest, including Folk Life Festival, Bumbershoot, and Bite of Seattle. Seafair is always eagerly anticipated, with its hydroplane races and Navy Blue Angels with their amazing aerial maneuvers. The Seattle International Film Festival is now one of the largest in North America, and draws movie buffs by the thousands. Beyond the city, there are wonderful festivals from the Victorian Festival of Port Townsend to the ever-popular Skagit Valley Tulip Festival. For festivals of film, *see also Film, p.54.*

March

Moisture Festival
Two weeks beginning late Mar; www.moisturefestival.com
Un-theatrical festival of comedy and variety, with jugglers, drill teams, vaudeville, and burlesque acts.

Victorian Festival
One weekend late Mar–May (varies annually); www.victorianfestival.org
Tours of historic Victorian homes, historical re-enactments, and Victorian fashion shows in Port Townsend on the Olympic Peninsula.

April

Skagit Valley Tulip Festival
Apr 1–30; www.tulipfestival.org
Field after field of glorious colorful tulips in the picturesque Skagit Valley, centered around Anacortes, Burlington, La Conner, and Mt Vernon.

May

Seattle Maritime Festival
2nd Sat May; www.seattle propellerclub.org
Come down to the Waterfront to watch the exciting tugboat races, sample great chowder, or go on a harbor tour.

Northwest Folk Life Festival
Memorial Day weekend; www.nwfolklife.org
Free celebration of folk and ethnic arts at the Seattle Center.

Public Holidays
Jan 1: New Year's Day
3rd Mon Jan: Martin Luther King, Jr Day
mid-Feb: Presidents' Day
last Mon in May: Memorial Day
July 4: Independence Day
1st Mon in Sept: Labor Day
2nd Mon in Oct: Columbus Day
Nov 11: Veterans' Day
4th Thur in Nov: Thanksgiving
Dec 25: Christmas

Left: Fourth of Jul-Ivar's fireworks and the Space Needle.

Seattle Children's International Festival
One week mid-May; www.seattleinternational.org
Art forms from around the globe for teens to tots, including theater groups, acrobats, musicians, and puppet shows.

Seattle International Film Festival (SIFF)
3rd week May–mid-June; www.seattlefilm.org
400-plus feature, documentary, and short films spread over 25 days.
SEE ALSO FILM, P.54

June

Fremont Summer Solstice Parade and Street Fair
Weekend closest to Jun 21; www.fremontfair.com
Zany, free-spirited parade featuring colorful floats, huge puppets, and naked cyclists. The Street Fair has tons of stalls offering food, drinks, arts and crafts.

Seattle Pride Festival
One Sun late Jun; www.seattle pride.org
The exuberant and enthusi-

Left: Bavarian fun at the Fremont Oktoberfest.

Chinatown-International District Summer Festival
One weekend mid-July; www.cidbia.org
Chinese, Japanese, Vietnamese, Filipino, and other Southeast Asian cultures celebrated with dragon dances, taiko drumming, wonderful food, and activities for all.

Sequim Lavender Festival
One weekend mid-July; www.lavenderfestival.com
Pick your own bouquet from fields of lavender in this sunny town located in the rain shadow of the Olympics Mountains.

August

Bumbershoot
Labor Day weekend; www.bumberhoot.org
This popular end-of-summer festival at the Seattle Center showcases film, music, and art.
SEE ALSO MUSIC, P.84

September

Puyallup Fair
Two weeks early Sept; www.thefair.com
Fairground rides, food halls, prize bunnies and hens, and competitions for best blueberry pie.

Fremont Oktoberfest
Third weekend in Sept; www.fremontoktoberfest.com
Beer, sausages, a fun run, chainsaw pumpkin-carving contest, and much more.

October

Earshot Jazz Festival
Two weeks mid-Oct; www.earshot.org
Top jazz performers from the Pacific Northwest and around the world.

Festal is a celebration of the diverse cultures from around the world that form part of the greater Seattle community. The free cultural events are held throughout the year at the Seattle Center, with music, dance, theater, food, arts, and crafts. Among the cultures celebrated are Vietnamese, African American, Irish, Japanese, Arab, Mexican, Turkish, Brazilian, Korean, and many others.

---

astic Gay Pride parade is held Downtown with inventive floats, colorful costumes, and lively music.

July

Seafair
Early July–early Aug; www.seafair.com
A range of events take place over the month, from the Downtown Torchlight Parade with the famous Seafair Pirates to hydroplane races on Lake Washington, with boats reaching speeds of over 150mph (240km/h), to the Navy Blue Angels doing daredevil formations in the sky above the lake.

WaMu Family Fourth
July 4; www.familyfourth.org
GasWorks Park is the best vantage point for Independence Day fireworks on Lake Union.

Fourth of Jul-Ivar's
July 4; www.ivars.net
To watch the Independence Day fireworks shooting off from Elliott Bay, Myrtle Edwards Park is the best place to be.

Bite of Seattle
One weekend mid-July; www.biteofseattle.com
The Seattle Center is the setting for tasting food from dozens of area restaurants.

Left: pick your own at the Sequim Lavender Festival.

Film

Every spring movie buffs flock to the Seattle International Film Festival, the largest film festival in North America, with more than 400 screenings. Smaller film festivals and events punctuate the calendar, but any day of the year independent as well as big-budget Hollywood productions can be seen at the city's original and distinctive movie theaters. Seattle is no stranger to starring in films, either, from the suspenseful assassination at the top of the Space Needle in *The Parallax View* (1974) to the re-enactment of the 1999 World Trade Organization riots in *Battle in Seattle* (2008).

Festivals and Forums

For three glorious weeks starting mid-May, the **Seattle International Film Festival (SIFF)** presents an astounding array of films across all genres from film-makers around the world, as well as showcasing some local tal-ent. Programs can be picked up at many coffee shops, bars, bookstores, and news-stands, and it's a good idea to get your ticket in advance because these events are seriously popular. Some screenings include Q&A with acclaimed directors. Events are held at cinemas through-out the city. The SIFF Cin-ema (McCaw Hall, 321 Mercer Street, Seattle Center; tel: 206-633-7151; www.seattlefilm.com; bus: 2, 3, 16; map p.130 B3) shows extraordinary films every day of the year.

Seattle has many more film festivals, including the **Children's Film Festival** (January), **Polish Film Festival** (April), **Jewish Film Festival** (April), and the **Gay and Lesbian Film Festival** (October).

The **Northwest Film Forum** (1515 12th Avenue, Capitol Hill; tel: 206-329-2629; www.nwfilmforum.org; bus: 10, 11, 12) is a non-profit organ-ization that supports local filmmakers with production and post-production facil-ities, workshops, and two cinemas.

Special Events

Some fun events to attend around town are the Silent Movie Mondays at the his-toric **Paramount Theatre** (911

Left: the front desk of the Harvard Exit Theatre.

Left: the Harvard Exit Landmark Theatre on Capitol Hill.

of the best venues for big films (90ft x 300ft/27m x 91m screen) and big audiences (seats more than 800).

Meridian 16
1501 7th Avenue, Downtown; tel: 206-223-9600; www.regal cinemas.com; bus: 10, 43, 49; map p.133 D3
A big Downtown multiplex showing the latest blockbusters and Hollywood hits.

Greater Seattle Area on Screen

IN THE MOVIES
It Happened at the World's Fair (1963)
The Parallax View (1974)
An Officer and a Gentleman (1982)
The Fabulous Baker Boys (1989)
Singles (1992)
Sleepless in Seattle (1993)
Hype (1996)
Snow Falling on Cedars (1999)
Battle in Seattle (2008)

ON TELEVISION
Twin Peaks (1990–1)
Northern Exposure (1990–95)
Frasier (1993–2004)
Grey's Anatomy (2005–)

If you'd rather enjoy your movies on your own, check out the staggering collection of rare, obscure, and hard-to-find films at awesome **Scarecrow Video**, the largest video store on the West Coast, with over 60,000 titles to rent, and thousands more for sale (5030 Roosevelt Way NE, University District; tel: 206-524-8554; www.scarecrowvideo.com; Sun–Thur 11am–11pm, Fri–Sat 11am–midnight; bus: 30, 66, 72).

Pine Street, Downtown; tel: 206-467-5510; www.theparamount. com; bus: 10, 12, 49), and cult classics at the **Fremont Outdoor Cinema** (N. 35th and Phinney Avenue, Fremont; tel: 206-781-4230; www.fremontoutdoor movies.com; bus: 26, 28) – bring something to sit on!

Movie Theaters

LANDMARK THEATRES
Part of the Landmark Theatres group, these historic movie theaters show a great selection of independent films, from art-house to foreign, documentaries to comedies to dramas. They have shared ticket and schedule information (tel: 206-781-5755; www.landmark theatres.com)

The Egyptian
805 E. Pine Street, Capitol Hill; bus: 11, 14, 49

Guild 45th Theatre
2115 N. 45th Street, Wallingford; bus: 16, 44

Harvard Exit
807 E. Roy Street, Capitol Hill; bus: 14, 49, 60

The Neptune
1303 NE 45th Street, University District; bus: 49, 66, 71

Varsity Theatre
4329 University Way NE, University District; bus: 43, 49, 72

OTHER MOVIE THEATERS

Cinerama
2100 4th Avenue, Belltown; tel: 206-441-3653; www.seattle cinerama.com; bus: 33, 39, 174
Microsoft co-founder Paul Allen saved this fabulous theater from the wrecking ball, and spruced it up to be one

Right: Twede's Cafe in North Bend, featured in the hit TV series *Twin Peaks*.

Food and Drink

Freshly caught fish, succulent seafood, farm-raised beef, and free-range poultry are the sorts of ingredients you'll find on menus and in kitchens throughout Seattle. Add to that organic seasonal vegetables, sun-kissed berries, and some fine artisan cheeses and breads and you get the idea of the wide choices available to consumers here. And the choices aren't limited to food; Washington wineries produce excellent vintages, and Seattle-area microbreweries produce handcrafted ales and stouts to quench your thirst. *See also Bars, p.28–33, Coffee Shops, p.36–41, and Restaurants, p.100–11. For food markets, see also Shopping, p.118–119.*

Seattle's Food Culture

Seattleites have developed discerning, educated palates thanks in part to the efforts of Tom Douglas, the celebrity chef who rose to prominence in the 1980s with the opening of Dahlia Lounge *(see p.100)*, setting a high standard for other chefs to follow. Nowadays it's common to see high-quality, locally sourced, sustainable ingredients on menus, with a strong emphasis on fish and seafood, from salmon to oysters and clams. Being surrounded by nature that produces everything from fresh fish to fabulous fruits, it's no wonder a whole host of young Seattle chefs are winning accolades.

Washington State Wine and Beer

Washington state is the nation's second-largest producer of wine (after California), and the number of wineries has quadrupled in the last decade to more than 500. The grapes are mostly nurtured on the eastern side of the Cascades, but a growing number are being processed by wineries in the Puget Sound region, including **Chateau Ste Michelle**, **Columbia Winery**, **Chatter Creek**, and **Cuillin Hills**.

Microbreweries exploded in the 1980s, and Seattle is home to many good ones, including **Pyramid Ales**, **Elysian Brewing Company**, **Redhook**, **Hale's Ales**, **Maritime Pacific**, **Elliott Bay Brewing Company**, and **Mac & Jack's**. The city's bars are well stocked with local brews; several of the breweries have restaurants or pubs attached. SEE ALSO BARS, P.32; RESTAURANTS, P.106–7

Specialty Food Stores

Pike Place Market *(see*

Left: Seattleites love seafood.

home-made cookies and cakes.

PCC Natural Market
600 N. 34th Street, Fremont; tel: 206-632-6811; www.pcc naturalmarkets.com; daily 6am–midnight; bus: 26, 28, 31
A branch of a supermarket specializing in organic, local, and sustainably grown food.

Seattle Fish Company
4435 California Avenue SW, West Seattle; tel: 206-938-7576; www.seattlefishcompany.com; daily 10am–7pm; bus: 55, 85
Specializing in all wild fish, the display cases present sashimi-grade ahi tuna, whole snapper, many other fish and shellfish in season, and the tastiest dungeoness crab cakes, halibut cakes, and salmon cakes.

Uwajimaya
600 5th Avenue S, International District; tel: 206-624-6248; www.uwajimaya.com; Mon–Sat 9am–10pm, Sun 9am–9pm; bus: 26, 42; map p.134 C2
Amazing Asian supermarket stocked with the freshest fish and shellfish, oriental baked goods, noodles galore, many kinds of soy sauce, teriyaki, and seasonings, and exotic fruits and vegetables. It also has a food court with the cuisine of many different Asian nations.
SEE ALSO RESTAURANTS, P.104

Got a sweet tooth? Satisfy that craving for sugar at one of the city's fab coffee shops that serve up doughnuts, cupcakes, scones, cookies, and other sweet surprises. *See also Coffee Shops, p.36–41.*
If it's chocolate you're after, be sure to visit **Theo's Chocolate** in Fremont at 3400 Phinney Avenue N. and go on a tour.

---

p.119) is the best starting point for any foraging expedition, with its exceptional selection of fish, meats, cheese, produce, and ethnic ingredients in the many specialty stores. Almost every neighborhood has a good bakery and interesting food stores, but some favorites are listed here.

DeLaurenti Specialty Food Market
1435 1st Avenue, Pike Place Market; tel: 206-622-0141; www.delaurenti.com; Mon–Sat 9am–6pm, Sun 10am–5pm;

bus: 10, 12, 15; map p.136 A3
Whether perfectly sliced Black Forest ham, a jar of Marmite, or Italian biscotti beckon you in, chances are you'll end up leaving with a full bag of irresistible European comestibles.

Olsen's Scandinavian Foods
2248 Market, Ballard; tel: 206-783-8288; www.scandinavian foods.net; Mon–Fri 9am–5pm, Sat 10am–5pm; bus: 44, 46
Run by the same family for nearly 50 years, Olsen's keeps Ballard residents supplied with pickled herring, fish cakes, potato lefse, and

Left: beer from the Elysian Brewing Company. **Right:** fresh fish at Pike Place Market; local produce at a farmers' market.

Gay and Lesbian

After San Francisco, Seattle has the second-highest gay and lesbian population of any city in the United States, making up 12.9 percent of the total population. The epicenter of gay and lesbian life in Seattle is the Capitol Hill neighborhood, where same-sex smooching and hand-holding doesn't turn a head. Businesses from bookstores to bars to churches cater to the gay market, with rainbow banners flying from many establishments. And although the annual Pride parade was moved to Downtown to accommodate larger crowds, Broadway is still at the center of the gay, lesbian, bisexual, and transgender community.

Bars and Clubs

Century Ballroom
2nd floor, 915 E. Pine, Capitol Hill; tel: 206-324-7263; www.centuryballroom.com; Tue–Sun 9pm–1am; bus: 9, 49, 60

Offering classes in queer swing and salsa, this lively ballroom has a very friendly vibe, and also offers regular outdancing events.

The Elite
1520 E. Olive Way, Capitol Hill; tel: 206-860-0999; daily noon–2am; bus: 8, 14, 43

In its second incarnation after 30 years on Broadway, The Elite is a classy gay bar with a pool table, a lounge with easy chairs, and video games upstairs. On game days, a mixed crowd streams in to watch the Seahawks.

Neighbours
1509 Broadway, Capitol Hill; tel: 206-324-5358; www.neighboursnightclub.com; Sun–Mon, Wed 4pm–2am, Thur 4pm–3am, Fri–Sat 4pm–4am; bus: 11, 49

Seattle's most famous gay nightclub, Neighbours is the place to glam up and get ready to dance the night away to disco, pop, and house music. A younger mixed gay and straight crowd, and drag queens too.

Purr Cocktail Lounge
1518 11th Avenue, Capitol Hill; tel: 206-325-3112; www.purrseattle.com; Mon–Sat 3pm–2am, Sun 2pm–midnight; bus: 10, 49

Strong cocktails, Mexican-themed food, and loud music in this chic, largely gay bar.

R Place
619 E. Pine Street, Capitol Hill; tel: 206-726-1824; www.rplaceseattle.com; Mon–Fri 4pm–2am, Sat–Sun 2pm–2am; bus: 11, 49

A cool crowd of gays, lesbians, and some straights come for the strong drinks, to dance upstairs, to join in

Left: a barman at Neighbours nightclub on Capitol Hill.

Left: a pick-up truck gets a Gay Pride Parade make-over.

Sat noon–5pm; bus: 4, 14, 48
A wide range of resources and support for Seattle's lesbian community.

Pride Foundation
tel: 206-323-3318; www.seattle pride.org
Among other things, this organization promotes events for the month-long **Seattle Pride** *(see p.52–3)*, which takes place in June. The website is also a great source of information for gay and lesbian events through the year.

Seattle Gay News
Published every Friday, this weekly LGBT newspaper covers news, the arts, entertainment, events, and classifieds. It is available at many Capitol Hill coffee shops, bars, and bookstores, or you can visit online at www.sgn.org.

Seattle LGBT Community Center
720 7th Avenue, First Hill; tel: 206-323-5428; www.seattle lgbt.org; Mon–Sat 10am–9pm, Sun 11am–8pm; bus: 3, 545
A health and human services agency that reaches out to the lesbian, gay, bisexual, and transgender community of Seattle through advocacy, support groups, and referrals.

Every October, Three Dollar Bill Cinema produces the annual **Seattle Gay and Lesbian Film Festival**, which brings queer films from around the world to the Pacific Northwest. Festival programs are available at many Capitol Hill bookstores, coffee shops, and movie theaters.

Thursday's amateur strip show, or to catch Friday's Queen Lucky spinning the hits.

Wildrose
1021 E. Pike Street, Capitol Hill; tel: 206-324-9210; www.thewild rosebar.com; Sun–Mon 3pm–1am, Tue–Sat 3pm–2am; bus: 11, 49
Popular lesbian bar and restaurant with special events like pool tournaments, trivia nights, karaoke, and live music.

Resources

Bailey-Coy Bookstore
414 Broadway E, Capitol Hill; tel: 206-323-8842; www.bailey coybooks.com; Mon–Sat

10am–10pm, Sun 10am–8pm; bus: 9, 49, 60
A good selection of gay and lesbian literature, knowledgeable staff, and a place for community notices.

Capitol Hill Travel
410 Broadway E, 110, Seattle, WA 98102 (mail address only); tel: 206-726-8998; www.capitol hilltravel.com
Vacation planning for gay and lesbian travelers.

Lesbian Resource Center
2214 S. Jackson Street, Central District; tel: 206-322-3953; www.lrc.net; Tue–Fri noon–7pm,

Right: Pride Festival attracts huge crowds to Downtown.

History

20,000 BC
Small bands of Ice Age hunters cross the Bering Land Bridge from Asia.

7000–1000 BC
Tribes of the Puget Sound region become dependent on fishing.

1792
English navigator Capt. George Vancouver lands near present-day Everett, north of Seattle. His expedition explores Puget Sound, named for Peter Puget, a lieutenant on Vancouver's crew.

1833
The Hudson's Bay Company establishes Fort Nisqually in present-day Tacoma.

1851
David Denny and a group of settlers arrive at Alki Point, in what is now West Seattle. They name their settlement Alki-New York.

1852
Disappointed by Alki Point's severe weather and poor port potential, Denny and his crew shift north to Elliott Bay, near present-day Seattle.

1853
The relocated town is laid out and named for Chief Sealth (Seattle), a friend of the settlers.

1854
A treaty with the local tribes provides for the newcomers to "buy" Indian land.

1855
Chief Seattle – leader of the Duwamish, Suquamish and other Puget Sound tribes – signs the Port Elliott treaty, giving away Indian land and establishing a reservation.

1856
Some Indians rebel against the treaty, but the rebellion is quickly supressed by the US Army.

1882
Flamed by the economic depression, animosity against Chinese immigrants increases.

1886
Racial violence breaks out against Chinese residents. Five men are shot, and Chinese stores and homes are destroyed. Two hundred Chinese are forced onto a San Francisco-bound ship.

1889
A handyman pours water onto a flaming pot of glue in a paint store. The resulting explosion and fire destroys the entire 60-block Downtown area of Seattle.

1893
The Great Northern Railway arrives, making Seattle a major rail terminus.

1897
The SS *Portland* sails into the city, carrying hundreds of thousands of dollars' worth of gold from the Yukon's Klondike. Seattle's mayor resigns and heads north for gold.

LATE 1890S
Japanese laborers begin arriving.

1900
In Tacoma, Midwesterner Frederick Weyerhaeuser buys 900,000 acres (360,000 hectares) of Pacific Northwest timberland unwanted by the Northern Pacific Railroad.

1909
The Alaska-Yukon-Pacific Exposition is held.

1916
The Lake Washington Ship Canal opens. William Boeing, a prosperous lumberman, incorporates the Pacific Aero Products Company; a year later it's renamed the Boeing Airplane Company.

1919
The country's first and longest general strike is held in Seattle; however, it becomes a tactical error as some of its supporters are targeted as Communists.

1941

The US entry into World War II invigorates Seattle's importance, both in shipbuilding and in aircraft manufacturing.

1942

6,000 Japanese-Americans are shipped from Seattle and placed in Idaho internment camps. James Marshall Hendrix, aka Jimi Hendrix, is born in Seattle.

1950

An economic recession is brought to an end by the Korean War; Seattle builds B-47 bombers.

1962

The Seattle World's Fair introduces the city – and the Space Needle – to the world.

1969

Boeing lays off 60 percent of its employees as the demand for commercial aircraft plummets. The city's economy heads into a tailspin.

1971

The first Starbucks opens, situated in Pike Place Market.

1979

Seattle's SuperSonics win the National Basketball Association (NBA) championship.

1980

After being dormant for almost 200 years, the volcano of Mt St Helens explodes to the south of Seattle.

1992

Seattle becomes a music center as grunge music – including Nirvana and Pearl Jam – sweeps the world.

1993

Forbes magazine rates Microsoft chairman Bill Gates as the richest man in the world.

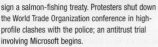

1999

Safeco Field replaces the Kingdome to host Major League baseball; Canada and the US sign a salmon-fishing treaty. Protesters shut down the World Trade Organization conference in high-profile clashes with the police; an antitrust trial involving Microsoft begins.

2001

The tech boom collapses. A riot erupts during Mardi Gras, and one man is killed. The next day, an earthquake measuring 6.8 on the Richter scale hits the area. Boeing moves its corporate headquarters to Chicago and many jobs are lost.

2002

Seahawks Stadium (now Qwest Field) opens for the NFL season. Seattle Central Community College is named College of the Year by *Time* magazine. Boeing's post-September 11 job losses hit 35,000. The US District Court conditionally approves a Microsoft antitrust settlement.

2003

Seattle-based Amazon.com turns its first profit after several years of trading.

2004

With women's national basketball, the city wins its first national sports title since 1979.

2005

Voters pass the strictest smoking ban in the US, prohibiting smoking in all workplaces, bars, and restaurants and within 25ft (7.6m) of doors and windows.

2006

Starbucks CEO Howard Schultz sells the Seattle SuperSonics basketball team to a group of Oklahoma City businessmen; the Seattle Seahawks (football) play their first Super Bowl; Seattle breaks a 73-year-old record for the most rain in one month (November).

2006

In March seven young people are killed by Kyle Huff, who opens fire on a house party in the city's Capitol Hill neighborhood. In July, armed gunman Naveed Haq storms into the Jewish Federation building, shooting six women, one of them fatally.

2007

The new Boeing Dreamliner 787 is taken on its first test flight in Everett, north of Seattle.

Hotels

Seattle's highest concentration of hotels is in Downtown, where they tend to be on the luxurious side, often with price tags to match. Other areas offer a good choice of accommodations, especially in terms of B&Bs and smaller hotels, and provide the opportunity to explore some characterful neighborhoods. Capitol Hill has a good concentration of B&Bs, and the U-District has hotels that appeal to students and their parents. West Seattle and Ballard both offer fresh sea air and beach parks nearby. Also listed are farther-flung accommodations for those making excursions into the Greater Puget Sound region.

Downtown and Belltown

Ace Hotel

2423 1st Avenue; tel: 206-448-4721; www.theacehotel.com; $–$$; bus: 15, 18, 22; map p.132 B4

A minimalist and futuristic small Downtown hotel in a historic building. Each room is different, but the common themes of white walls, white floors, and simplicity pervade. Rooms are available with shared or private bathrooms, but each has a sink and vanity. The attention to detail includes beds made with wool French army blankets.

The Alexis

1007 1st Avenue; tel: 206-624-4844; www.alexishotel.com; $$$; bus: 10, 12, 18; map p.133 D1

Located in an early 20th-century building near the waterfront, this elegant boutique hotel prides itself on attention to detail. Throughout the hotel are works of art by Northwest artists. The rooms are richly decorated; opt for one facing the courtyard, because those facing 1st Avenue tend to be noisy. Unwind in front of a fireplace, and enjoy a complimentary glass of sherry. Continental breakfast included.

Arctic Club Hotel

700 3rd Avenue; tel: 206-340-0340; www.arcticclubhotel.com; $$$; bus: 3, 11, 28; map p.134 B4

Opened in 2008, this luxury Downtown hotel occupies the historic Arctic Building,

> Price for a standard double room in high season (not including breakfast):
> $$$ More than $200
> $$ $100–199
> $ Under $100

Bed & breakfasts offer a more homey and personal stay than most hotels. A selection of B&Bs is included in these listings, but for more information contact **Seattle Bed & Breakfast Inn Association** (tel: 206-547-1020 or 1-800-348-5630) or **Pacific Bed & Breakfast Registry** (tel: 206-439-7677 or 1-800-684-2932; www.seattle bedandbreakfast.com).

designed as an exclusive men's club for the Klondike gold prospectors who struck it rich. Lovingly restored original features, such as the historic Northern Lights Dome Room with its striking ceiling and the foyer lined with Alaskan marble. Expect to be pampered, and enjoy the amenities that include whirlpool tubs, Kiehl's toiletries, free WiFi, and a fitness center.

Days Inn Town Center
2205 7th Avenue; tel: 206-448-3434; www.daysinntownscenter.com; $; bus: 5, 25, 26; map p.131 C1
A Downtown bargain with clean, affordable rooms within walking distance of the Space Needle and Seattle Center. Parking is available for a fee, but the hotel is within the Metro ride-free zone, making bus travel to many sites easy.

The Edgewater
2411 Alaskan Way, Pier 67; tel: 206-728-7000 or 1-800-624-0670; www.edgewaterhotel.com; $$–$$$; bus: 99; map p.132 A3
Built at the time of the World's Fair in 1962 and completely remodeled in 1989, this is Seattle's only Downtown waterfront hotel. It stands right on Pier 67. It shot to prominence in 1964 when The Beatles stayed here and famously fished from their window. Current amenities include an atrium lobby, stone fireplaces, and mountain-lodge décor. Complimentary Downtown shuttle.

Executive Hotel Pacific
400 Spring Street; tel: 1-800-426-1165; www.pacificplaza hotel.com; $$; bus: 2, 12, 66; map p.133 D2
Boutique-sized hotel next door to the modern steel-and-glass Seattle Central Library, it was built in 1928, and renovations in 2004 preserved its charm while updating the facilities and décor. The rooms are classy, with cherry wood and leather touches, and gold- and green-toned furnishings. It's also pet-friendly. On site is the Jasmine restaurant.

The Fairmont Olympic Hotel
411 University Street; tel: 206-621-1700 or 1-800-223-8772;

63

www.fairmont.com; $$$; bus: 2, 3, 70; map p.133 D2
The grande dame of Seattle hotels, the Olympic was built in the Italian Renaissance style in 1924 and is listed on the National Register of Historic Places. The public spaces are gracious and elegant, and the spacious guest rooms are furnished with period reproductions. Enjoy high tea in the atrium-style Garden Court and luxury shopping off the lobby. The hotel receives the AAA five-diamond award for service.

Green Tortoise Hostel
105 Pike Street; tel: 206-340-1222; www.greentortoise.net; $; bus: 10, 15, 18; map p.136 A3
This hostel at Pike Place Market offers dorm-style accommodations at very reasonable prices; there are also some private rooms. Free

computer terminals (and free WiFi). Continental breakfast included daily; dinner three times a week. Wednesday is Open Mic Night, with a variety of performers.
Hotel 1000
1000 1st Avenue; tel: 206-957-1000 or 1-877-315-1088;

Price for a standard double room in high season (not including breakfast):	
$$$	More than $200
$$	$100–199
$	Under $100

Left: Hotel Ändra.

www.hotel1000seattle.com; $$$; bus: 10, 16, 66; map p.133 D1

In one of the city's newer hotels, technology is employed in inventive ways to ensure a memorable, comfortable stay. The smart and stylish guest rooms feature flat-screen TVs, sensors in the minibar to alert staff when it's time to restock, bathtubs that fill from the ceiling, and the opportunity to select your own artwork. Venture out of your room to enjoy the restaurant **boka**, or relax at the virtual golf club (where you can simulate play on some of the world's best courses), or have an indulging treatment at the Spaahh.

SEE ALSO RESTAURANTS, P.100

Hotel Ändra

2000 4th Avenue; tel: 206-448-8600 or 1-877-448-8600; www.hotelandra.com; $$–$$$; bus: 1, 42, 70; map p.133 C3

Housed in an original 1926 brick building, the Hotel Ändra is designed in Northwest/Scandinavian style in a prime Belltown location. The rooms have luxurious furnishings, from goose-down comforters and pillows to Egyptian cotton linens and Swedish toiletries. One of the shining lights in Seattle cuisine, Tom Douglas, has his Lola restaurant on the main floor of the hotel.

Hotel Max

620 Stewart Street; tel: 206-728-6299 or 1-866-833-6299; www.hotelmaxseattle.com; $$$; bus: 70; map p.133 D3

This stylish hotel specializes in original art throughout. The Max attracts a hip crowd, but the easy welcome and low-

Left and right: the lobby and entrance to Hotel Monaco.

key service mean that everyone feels at home. With comfy beds and millions of movies on the in-room plasma screens, if you stay here you might never see the rest of Seattle. For excellent sushi, try **Red Fin**, the adjoining restaurant.

SEE ALSO RESTAURANTS, P.103

Hotel Monaco

1101 4th Avenue; tel: 206-621-1770 or 1-800-945-2240; www.monaco-seattle.com; $$$; bus: 2, 66, 125; map p.133 D2

A recent addition to Seattle's hotel scene, this boutique hotel with rich colors, bold patterns (including striped wallpaper), and lots of textures makes a change from many more staid hotels. Lots of pleasant touches, such as robes and nice toiletries, and eco-friendly cleaning products. The hotel restaurant is the Southern-inspired Sazerac.

Hotel Vintage Park

1100 5th Avenue; tel: 206-624-8000 or 1-800-624-4433; www.hotelvintagepark.com; $$$; bus: 2, 13; map p.133 D2

Wine-lovers will be drawn to this boutique hotel, whose guest rooms are all named after local wineries and vineyards. There's also a nightly wine reception, which

> For those on a tight budget who don't mind roughing it, there are a couple of hostels with dorm-style accommodations at very low rates: **Green Tortoise Hostel** (Downtown, *see left*) or **Hostel Seattle** (Ballard, *see p.69*). Be sure to reserve these in advance.

SEE ALSO RESTAURANTS, P.102

Left: Hotel Vintage Park on 5th Avenue.

King's Inn
2106 5th Avenue; tel: 206-441-8833; www.kingsinnseattle.com; $$; bus: 39, 42, 70; map p.133 C4

This Belltown motel offers basic accommodations and free parking, with a great central location alongside the monorail tracks that connect Downtown with the Seattle Center. There is no restaurant on-site, but there are plenty of restaurants and coffee shops in the neighborhood, including **Top Pot**, with its doughnuts, virtually next door.
SEE ALSO COFFEE SHOPS, P.37

Mayflower Park Hotel
405 Olive Way; tel: 206-623-8700 or 1-800-426-5100; www.mayflowerpark.com; $$$; bus: 2, 43, 49; map p.133 D3

A moderately sized European-style hotel, the Mayflower Park is in a tastefully restored 1927 building with elegant touches including crystal chandeliers. It has a prime location for shopping and sightseeing, being adjacent to Westlake Center and within easy walking distance of Pike Place Market. Downstairs is the Mediterranean-style restaurant Andaluca.

Moore Hotel
1926 2nd Avenue; tel: 206-448-4851 or 1-800-421-5508; www.moorehotel.com; $; bus: 2, 15, 33; map p.133 C3

This basic hotel is connected to the historic Moore Theatre and is on the fringe of countless bars and restaurants in Belltown. Even more economical European-style rooms are available if you're willing to walk down the hall

features wines from across Washington state. Guest rooms are decorated in vintage style with rich colors and a touch of luxury. The restaurant, **Tulio**, serves authentic Italian food.
SEE ALSO RESTAURANTS, P.102

Inn at Harbor Steps
1221 1st Avenue; tel: 206-748-0973 or 1-888-728-8910; www.innatharborsteps.com; $$$; bus: 10, 12, 15; map p.133 C1

Part of a hotel chain based in California called 'Four Sisters,' this small hotel is geared toward country-inn experiences. Each room at the inn has a fireplace, a wet bar, and a sitting area. Amenities include a sauna, Jacuzzi, and indoor pool along with complimentary hors d'oeuvres and wine before dinner. Full breakfast is included.

Inn at the Market
86 Pine Street; tel: 206-443-3600; www.innatthemarket.com; $$$; bus: 10, 15, 22; map p.136 A2

Located in the Pike Place Market, many of the rooms have splendid views of Elliott Bay. The inn surrounds a quiet landscaped courtyard that has shops, a spa, and a very good restaurant, **Campagne**, serving French country cuisine. A fifth-floor deck offers one of the best views in town.
SEE ALSO RESTAURANTS, P.102

Price for a standard double room in high season (not including breakfast):
$$$	More than $200
$$	$100–199
$	Under $100

Right: the lobby at the Inn at the Harbor Steps.

to a shared bathroom. Most rooms are a good size, but don't expect any frills.

Roosevelt Hotel

1531 7th Avenue; tel: 206-621-1200; www.roosevelthotel.com; $$$; bus: 49, 70; map p.133 D3

The Art Deco Roosevelt was built in 1930, and the attractive exterior is crowned at night by the hotel's name in red neon letters. Rooms are small, but the mid-sized hotel is central to shopping, Downtown sightseeing, and the Washington State Convention Center. Von's Grand City Café serves good food and a mean Martini.

W Seattle

1112 4th Avenue; tel: 206-264-6000; www.starwoodhotels.com; $$$; bus: 2, 13; map p.133 D2

Voted one of the 100 sexiest hotels in the world, the W Seattle has a cool, contemporary, minimalist style. The Earth & Ocean restaurant has won accolades, while the W Bar is great for flirting over cocktails. There's a business center, a 'sweatness' center, and an in-room spa service. Even pets are pampered.

Some of the higher-end business hotels offer good weekend rates to entice more customers. It is always worth asking whether any discounts or special offers are available when booking your hotel.

Westin Hotel

1900 5th Avenue; tel: 206-728-1000 or 1-800-228-3000; www.westin.com; $$$; bus: 70, South Lake Union Streetcar; map p.133 D3

With two distinctive circular towers *(see picture, p.68)*, this is the Westin chain's flagship hotel, adjacent to the Westlake Shopping Center and convenient for the monorail, South Lake Union Streetcar, and the attractions of Downtown. The rooms are coveted and spacious, with views of Puget Sound or the city, and there's a large pool.

Pioneer Square and the International District

Best Western Pioneer Square Hotel

77 Yesler Way; tel: 206-340-1234 or 1-800-800-5514; www. pioneersquarehotel.com; $$–$$$; bus: 16, 99; map p.134 B4

This mid 19th-century hotel is listed on the National Register of Historic Places. The location is perfect for the art galleries and boutiques of the Pioneer Square neighborhood, and it's convenient to the Safeco Field for baseball, or Qwest Field for football or any of the big shows held there. Continental breakfast is included.

Seattle Center and Lower Queen Anne

Inn at Queen Anne

505 1st Avenue N; tel: 206-282-7357 or 1-800-952-5043; www.innatqueenanne.com; $$; bus: 1, 2, 15; map p.130 A3

Near the Seattle Center and the restaurants, bars, and stores of Lower Queen Anne, this economical 1930s hotel has more of a neighborhood feel than many hotels. Continental breakfast is included, and each guest room also has a kitchenette. The hotel is not wheelchair-accessible.

MarQueen Hotel

600 Queen Anne Avenue N; tel: 206-282-7407 or 1-888-

Left: the distinctive towers of the Westin Hotel, *see p.67.*

There's a grand piano in the living room, a library with leaded glass, and a patio for relaxing.

Bed & Breakfast on Broadway

722 Broadway Avenue E; tel: 206-329-8933; www.bbon broadway.com; $$; bus: 9, 49

This attractive, tastefully furnished older home has two spacious guest rooms with queen beds and private baths, just one block from neighborhood shops, restaurants, coffee shops, and the independent Harvard Exit movie theater *(see p.55)*. The elegant parlor has a grand piano, hardwood floor, and oriental rugs.

Bed and Breakfast on Capitol Hill

739 Broadway Avenue E; tel: 206-325-0320; www.bbcapitolhill.com; $–$$; bus: 9, 49

A comfortable home built in 1903 in the Harvard-Belmont Historical District with three guest rooms (one with private bath), each with an antique bed and other homely touches. There is also a resident dog and cat. There is a minimum stay of two nights.

Gaslight Inn and Howell Street Suites

1727 15th Avenue; tel: 206-325-3654; www.gaslight-inn.com; $–$$; bus: 10

This early 20th-century mansion has eight attractive guest rooms, each decorated in a different style; some share a bathroom. Outside is a large pool, which is heated in the summer months. The proprietors are friendly and aim to please. No kids, pets, or smoking.

445-3076; www.marqueen.com; $$$; bus: 1, 2, 15; map p.130 A3

This elegant boutique hotel is conveniently located next to the Seattle Center in the bustling Lower Queen Anne neighborhood. The historic building dates from 1918, and the guest rooms are well appointed with robes, quality toiletries, and kitchens.

Travelodge Space Needle

200 6th Avenue N; tel: 206-441-7878 or 1-800-578-7878; www.travelodge.com/seattle 07033; $$; bus: 358; map p.130 C2

Price for a standard double room in high season (not including breakfast):	
$$$	More than $200
$$	$100–199
$	Under $100

Convenient to Seattle Center and the Space Needle, this economical choice includes free parking, continental breakfast, and WiFi. There is a swimming pool and Jacuzzi to relax in after a day's sight-seeing. The facilities have been upgraded recently, and the hotel is a smoke-free facility.

Capitol Hill

Bacon Mansion

959 Broadway E, tel: 206-329-1864 or 1-800-240-1864; www.baconmansion.com; $–$$; bus: 9, 49

This mock Tudor mansion in the historic Harvard-Belmont Landmark District has 11 rooms, five with private baths. There is also a carriage house on the grounds, which is perfect for a family or a group touring together.

Right: the entrance to Capitol Hill's elegant Salisbury House.

Hill House B&B

1113 E. John Street; tel: 206-323-4455; www.seattlehill
house.com; $–$$; bus: 8
Built in 1903, this restored Victorian house has five elegantly decorated rooms, three with private baths. Breakfast, cooked by the innkeeper, can be a gourmet experience. Guests can rest from the exertions of the day in the living room or on the back porch overlooking the garden. There's a minimum stay of two or three nights.

Mildred's Bed & Breakfast

1202 15th Avenue E; tel: 206-325-6072 or 1-800-327-9692; www.mildredsbnb.com; $–$$; bus: 10
Four guest rooms with private baths, some with skylights or views of nearby Volunteer Park. The home was built in 1890, and the proprietors have furnished it in Victorian style. There's a putting green on the front lawn, and visitors can also relax on the wraparound porch. This leafy residential neighborhood has a cluster of coffee shops, restaurants, and bars, and it's just a short walk to Broadway.

Salisbury House

750 16th Avenue E; tel: 206-328-8682; www.salisbury
house.com; $$; bus: 10
Located in a historic neighborhood near Volunteer Park, Salisbury House (built in 1904) greets visitors with an inviting wraparound porch. The interior is just as special as its elegant surroundings, with four well-appointed guest rooms (each with private bathroom) on the second floor, and a suite with its own private entrance on the ground floor. Tasty vegetarian breakfasts.

Shafer-Baillie Mansion

907 14th Avenue E; tel: 206-322-4654 or 1-800-985-4654; www.sbmansion.com; $$; bus: 10
This Tudor mansion is set within spacious grounds in a quiet, upscale neighborhood, just a block from Volunteer Park. Gourmet breakfasts, antique furnishings, and wood paneling add to the atmosphere. The three guest rooms and two suites all have private bathrooms and are appointed with quality furnishings and attention to detail.

Ballard

Hostel Seattle

6200 Seaview Avenue NW; tel: 206-706-3255 or 1-877-846-7835; www.hostelseattle.com; $; bus: 46
A relative newcomer to the Seattle lodging scene, this Ballard hostel has amazing views and a great location near Golden Gardens park. The friendly establishment is near all the sights of Ballard, the beautiful Puget Sound, and is accessible by bus to many other parts of the city.

West Seattle

Chittenden House

5649 47th Avenue SW; tel: 206-935-0407; www.chittenden
house.com; $$; bus: 22, 53, 54
This B&B is housed within a typical northwest craftsman-style home, with two guest rooms and one suite. It is located in the Junction neighborhood of West Seattle, which has a cluster of shops, restaurants, coffee shops, and bars, and is also close to Alki Beach and Lincoln Park. From the deck there are views of Puget Sound, and there is also a pleasant garden for guests to relax in.

Minimum two-night stay on weekends and holidays.

Villa Heidelberg
4845 45th Avenue SW; tel: 206-938-3658 or 1-800-671-2942; www.villaheidelberg.com; $$–$$$; bus: 22, 54, 55
From this West Seattle B&B there are great views of Puget Sound and the Olympic Mountains. The 1909 crafts-man home with a wrap-around porch is furnished with many original features, including a lovely wooden staircase, wooden beams and moldings, and leaded-glass windows. There are six guest rooms, with down comforters and bathrobes. Two of the rooms have pri-vate baths, the others share

two baths. Delicious gourmet breakfasts are served.

Other Great Neighborhoods

FIRST HILL
Sorrento Hotel
900 Madison Street; tel: 206-622-6400 or 1-800-426-1265; www.hotelsorrento.com; $$$; bus: 12
Just up the hill from Down-town, this 1909 hotel was modeled on a castle in Sor-rento, Italy. Guest rooms are sophisticated and stylish, yet due to its moderate size, the hotel offers an attentive ser-vice. During summer guests can dine alfresco in the courtyard, and afternoon tea is served daily in the fireside room.

SOUTH LAKE UNION
Residence Inn by Marriott
800 Fairview Avenue N; tel: 206-624-6000; www.marriott.com; $$$; bus: 66, 70, South Lake Union Streetcar

A large, all-suite hotel, this is a good choice for families and for those on longer visits, since each is equipped with a full kitchen (but the inn takes care of the dishes!). The majority of rooms overlook attractive Lake Union, and the South Lake Union Street-car can whisk you to Down-town in no time.

UNIVERSITY DISTRICT
Chambered Nautilus Bed and Breakfast Inn
5005 22nd Avenue NE; tel: 206-522-2536; www.chambered nautilus.com; $$; bus: 25, 74
This early 20th-century Geor-gian colonial-style hotel near the University of Washington has six rooms furnished with antiques and private baths. Four of the rooms open onto porches that have views of the Cascade Mountains. Amenities are lavish, includ-ing flowers, robes, bottled water, writing desks, and reading material taken from

Price for a standard double room in high season (not including breakfast):
$$$ More than $200
$$ $100–199
$ Under $100

Left and right: the Sorrento
Hotel's exterior and rooms.

the 2,000-plus books from
the library.

College Inn
4000 University Way NE;
tel: 206-633-4441;
www.collegeinnseattle.com; $;
bus: 49, 70, 71
In a historic building complex across from the University of Washington, this
small hostel-like hotel sits
above the popular College
Inn Pub and Café Allegro
(can be a little noisy). The
rooms, with shared baths,
are modest, but so are the
rates, and it's very convenient for the restaurants, bars,
and cinemas of the U-District
and for the University's
museums.

University Inn
4140 Roosevelt Way NE; tel: 206-
632-5055 or 1-800-733-3855;
www.universityinnseattle.com;
$$; bus: 66, 67, 79
This remodeled hotel is a
well-run addition to the U-
District, with an outdoor
swimming pool and a shuttle
service to many of the
tourist sights within the city.
Right next to the hotel, the
Portage Bay Café has a ter-
rific breakfast menu worth
getting up for.

Watertown
4242 Roosevelt Way NE;
tel: 206-826-4242 or 1-866-944-
4242; www.watertownseattle.
com; $$; bus: 66, 67, 79
Convenient to the University
of Washington, this sister
property to the University Inn
has comfortable rooms furnished with bathrobes and
Aveda toiletries. Other features are the evening wine-
tasting on weekdays, free
loaner bikes (perfect for the
nearby Burke-Gilman Trail),
and complimentary shuttle
service to the Seattle Center
and other sites.

Greater Seattle Area and Excursions

EAST OF SEATTLE

Mrs Anderson's Lodging House
917 Commercial Street, Leavenworth; tel: 1-800-253-8990;
www.quiltersheaven.com; $
The original Mrs Anderson is
long since gone, but this
cozy little inn has many a historical relic. The downstairs is
set up like a small museum,
and there are quilts, vintage
clothing, and historic photos
throughout. The rooms are
basic and small but clean,
and continental breakfast is
included.

Salish Lodge
6501 Railroad Avenue, Snoqualmie; tel: 1-800-272-5474;
www.salishlodge.com; $$$
At the top of Snoqualmie
Falls is this luxuriously
appointed lodge, where each
romantic room has a
whirlpool tub and wood-
burning fireplace, and many
have balconies, too. The spa

71

has therapeutic soaking pools, a steam room, and sauna for use by all guests, and additional treatments are available by appointment.

Willows Lodge
14580 NE 145th Street, Woodinville; tel: 425-424-3900 or 1-877-424-3930; www.willowslodge.com; $$$
A luxurious Northwest-style lodge bordering the Sammamish River, Willows Lodge is adjacent to the Redhook Brewery, Chateau Ste Michelle and Columbia wineries and perfect for wine-lovers. Food-lovers don't miss out, either, thanks to the splendid Herbfarm Restaurant on the grounds, which serves nine-course gourmet dinners.

Woodmark Hotel
1200 Carillon Point, Kirkland; tel: 425-822-3700; www.the woodmark.com; $$$

If you are a light sleeper, request a quiet room away from traffic or other street noise. Some of the older hotels and smaller hotels may be located in neighborhoods where late-night bars or clubs could keep you from getting your 40 winks.

This mid-sized hotel occupies an enviable setting on Lake Washington, in a ritzy 31-acre (12.5-hectare) shopping/office complex. Carillon Point also features a marina and the popular Ristorante Stresa, Yarrow Bay Restaurant and Beach Café, plus the Library Bar for afternoon tea served on bone china, surrounded by books.

SOUTH OF SEATTLE
Alexander's Country Inn
37515 Highway 706 E, Ashford; tel: 360-569-2300; www. alexanderscountryinn.com; $$
Located a mile from the Nisqually entrance to Mt Rainier National Park, this peaceful Victorian inn offers guests a cinema room with DVDs, a games room, an outdoor hot tub, and a rather tranquil setting where it's not uncommon to see deer nibbling in the grounds. The restaurant serves good, hearty meals.

National Park Inn & Paradise Inn
Mt Rainier National Park; tel: 360-569-2275; http://rainier. guestservices.com; $$
These two historic inns within the National Park provide

accommodations in truly stunning surroundings. The smaller National Park Inn near the Nisqually entrance is open year-round. The rustic Paradise Inn, at one of the park's most popular sites, offers marvelous views, plus a restaurant and café. It is open May–September, weather permitting.

WEST OF SEATTLE
Kalaloch Lodge
157151 Highway 101, Forks; tel: 1-866-525-2562; www.visit kalaloch.com; $$
Perched on a bluff overlooking the rugged Pacific Ocean, you can enjoy superb sunsets, long walks on the sandy beach strewn with driftwood, or hikes in the majestic Olympic National Park during your stay at Kalaloch. Choose from cabins, camping, or a room in the main lodge.

Lake Quinault Lodge
345 South Shore Road, Lake Quinault; tel: 360-288-2900 or 1-800-562-6672; www.visit lakequinault.com; $$–$$$
In a stunning setting on the shores of Lake Quinault on the Olympic Peninsula, this lodge is a National Historic Landmark. It is perfect for rest,

Left and above: the Salish Lodge at the top of Snoqualmie Falls.

relaxation, and recreation, near the Hoh Rainforest and the Olympic National Park. There is a restaurant on-site.

The James House
1238 Washington Street, Port Townsend; tel: 1-800-385-1238; www.jameshouse.com; $$

This elegant Victorian mansion in charming Port Townsend offers 10 guest rooms (all en suite) furnished with antiques and most with views. The house is set on a bluff overlooking the water, and there are splendid views from the garden, too. For a treat, splash out and reserve the beautifully furnished master suite. Full breakfast, cookies, and evening sherry are included.

NORTH OF SEATTLE

Fairhaven Village Inn
1200 10th Street, Bellingham; tel: 360-733-1311 or 1-877-733-1100; http://fairhaven villageinn.com; $$

This lovely inn lies in the heart of Bellingham's historic Fairhaven District, which is full of delightful bookstores, boutiques, and good restaurants. The historic inn has high ceilings, beautiful woodwork, and spacious rooms, some with fireplace or water view, and makes for a relaxing stay.

Gatsby Mansion
309 Belleville Street, Victoria, British Columbia, Canada; tel: 1-800-563-9656; www.gatsbymansion.com; $$

Conveniently close to the Inner Harbour and the Victoria Clipper pier, this lovely white inn is a good base for exploring charming Victoria. Rooms are in three historic buildings, which have elegant Victorian features of stained glass, imposing wooden staircase, and rich decoration. Fine restaurant, too.

Heron Inn
117 Maple Avenue, La Conner; tel: 360-466-4626; www.the heron.com; $$

In a pretty setting at the edge of La Conner is this small country-style inn with individually decorated guest rooms. On-site is the Watergrass Day Spa, for you to indulge in a pampering treatment. Be sure to book early for visits during April's Skagit Valley Tulip Festival *(see p.52)*.

Inn at Roche Harbor
PO Box 4001, Roche Harbor, San Juan Island; www.rocheharbor.com; $$–$$$

This lovely historic waterfront property offers a range of accommodations, from historic rooms with views to more modern cottages and suites. Guests can indulge with spa treatments, and there are several dining options.

Tucker House
260 B Street, Friday Harbor, San Juan Island; tel: 360-378-2783 or 1-800-965-0123; www.tucker house.com; $$

Located in the busy little port of Friday Harbor, the Tucker House complex, with little gardens and a range of cottages, is a quaint place to stay. The rooms are well appointed, with luxurious bathrooms including double Jacuzzi tubs in most rooms, and the owners provide home-cooked breakfast. The sister property, Harrison Suites, offers all-suites accommodations.

Price for a standard double room in high season (not including breakfast):
$$$ More than $200
$$ $100–199
$ Under $100

Industry

Mention Seattle's businesses, and software engineering giant Microsoft, aerospace manufacturer Boeing, and gourmet coffee retailer Starbucks spring to mind. But many other businesses across a wide range of industries make up the unique economic blend of the Puget Sound region. Health care and biomedical research are some of the best in the country, the Port of Seattle manages a huge import and export operation, and the retail and service sectors employ great numbers of people. Among the region's top public companies are wholesaler Costco, Washington Mutual Bank, and Amazon.com online retailer.

Health Care and Biomedical Research

Health care is a big deal in Seattle, since it accounts for close to 100,000 jobs in the city's hospitals, health-care services, and biomedical research industry. The city has one of the nation's highest concentrations of biotechnology research, centered around South Lake Union, with organizations like **Fred Hutchinson Cancer Research Center**, or 'the Hutch,' **ZymoGenetics**, **UW Medicine**, the University of Washington's **Department of Global Health**, and the **Seattle Biomedical Research Institute**.

Aerospace Engineering

Although **Boeing's** headquarters are no longer in Seattle, the company founded in 1916 by lumberman Bill Boeing still plays a significant role in the economy. Its planes, and the parts they are comprised of, are made in huge plants throughout the region. The 787 Dreamliners are being assembled at the Everett plant, 25 miles (40km) north of the city. Daily tours of the

Future of Flight are also offered here (8415 Paine Field Blvd, Mukilteo; tel: 360-756-0086; www.futureofflight.org; daily between 8.30am–5.00pm; children must be 4ft/1.22m tall). The excellent **Museum of Flight** provides a thorough history of this aerospace and defense-industry giant.

SEE ALSO MUSEUMS AND GALLERIES, P.80–81

Information Technology

Altogether nearly 200,000 people in Washington state are employed in the IT sector across 3,000 companies. The software titan **Microsoft** is headquartered in the Eastside city of Redmond, where it also carries out research

and development. It employs more than 35,000 people in Washington state, and some 78,000 worldwide. Its campuses are closed to the public and guarded around the clock, but you can learn more

Non-profits have a strong presence in the region, from Christian aid organization **World Vision**, based in Federal Way (south of Seattle) to **The Bill & Melinda Gates Foundation**. In June 2008 Bill Gates stepped down from day-to-day operations at Microsoft to devote more time and energy to his foundation, which is dedicated to global health and education.

Left: a neighborhood branch of the coffee giant Starbucks.

Seattle has one of the most highly educated workforces in the country, with nearly 92 percent of students graduating from high school, and almost 53 percent of residents over the age of 25 holding a bachelor's degree. The major universities and colleges include the public **University of Washington** (the city's largest employer, with 28,000 faculty and staff), the network of **Seattle Community Colleges**, and the private **Seattle University**, **Seattle Pacific University**, the **Art Institute of Seattle**, and **Cornish College for the Performing Arts**.

Left: Microsoft's sprawling headquarters in Redmond.

about the company's history at the **Microsoft Visitor Center** (4420 148th Avenue NE, Redmond; tel: 425-703-6214; Mon–Fri 9am–7pm).

Although the software giant dominates Redmond, video-game company **Nintendo of America** has its headquarters for the Western Hemisphere right down the street, and to complete the tech trio, search-engine giant **Google** moved into nearby Kirkland in 2004.

Service and Retail

Seattleites and their cup of coffee go hand in hand, not surprising in a city that spawned gourmet coffee chain **Starbucks**, along with some much smaller competitors such as **Tully's**. The service and retail sector includes some other big names, such as wholesaler **Costco**, upscale department store **Nordstrom**, and outdoor out-

Right: Nintendo is also based in Redmond.

fitter **REI**. The online retailer **Amazon.com** also has its headquarters in the city.
SEE ALSO OUTDOOR ACTIVITIES, P.91; SHOPPING, P.116

Military

Several key military bases are spread throughout the Puget Sound region, making the US Defense Department one of the largest regional employers. Bases include the Naval Station in Everett, Fort Lewis Army Base and McChord Air Force Base (both south of Tacoma), and Bremerton's Puget Sound Naval Shipyard and Bangor Naval Submarine Base.

International Trade

Seattle is one of the top 10 container ports in the United States, with 500 acres (200 hectares) of space, a staggering 26 container cranes, and truck and rail links via Burlington Northern and Union Pacific to the rest of the country. Exports originating in Washington state and bound for the Pacific Rim countries (China, Japan, Korea, Taiwan), Europe, and Canada include aircraft parts, cereals and grains, wood and paper. Imports include cars, clothing, and consumer goods.

Museums and Galleries

For a city its size, Seattle has a diverse range of quality museums. Whether your interest lies in Asian art or in aviation, in science fiction or in sailing, you're bound to find a museum or gallery to suit you. Art highlights include the recently expanded and renovated Seattle Art Museum, while the Henry Art Gallery is a more intimate space. No visit to Seattle is complete without exploring the history of the Boeing Company at the Museum of Flight, and for music fans the Experience Music Project is the place to be.

Downtown and Belltown

Seattle Art Museum
1300 1st Avenue, Downtown; tel: 206-654-3100; www.seattle artmuseum.org; Tue–Wed, Sat–Sun 10am–5pm, Thur–Fri 10am–10pm; admission charge; bus: 23, 66, 150; map p.133 D2
A major expansion in 2007 provided much more space for SAM's permanent collection, and gave it the capacity to attract large national and international traveling exhibitions. Galleries in the museum are devoted to collections that include ancient Mediterranean and Islamic

art, Italian Renaissance paintings, decorative arts, Australian Aboriginal art, Korean and Japanese art including a traditional teahouse, traditional Pacific Northwest tribal art, American art, and modern art. In 2006, SAM's **Olympic Sculpture Park** opened at the north end of Downtown.
SEE ALSO PARKS, GARDENS, AND BEACHES P.97

Pioneer Square and the International District

Bill Speidel's Underground Tour
608 1st Avenue, Pioneer Square; tel: 206-682-4646; www.under

groundtour.com; several tours a day (between the hours of 10am–6pm in summer, 11am–3pm in winter); admission charge; bus: 73, 150, 194; map p.134 B4
While not a museum, this popular 90-minute guided tour provides a glimpse into Seattle's raucous roots, complete with opium dens, brothels, and saloons aplenty. The tour starts at **Doc Maynard's Public House**, a restored saloon from the 1890s, and then

Right: Klondike Gold Rush National Historic Park.

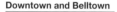

Best Museums for Art
Henry Art Gallery *(see p.80)*
Seattle Art Museum *(see above)*
Seattle Asian Art Museum *(see p.79)*
Best Museums for History
Klondike Gold Rush National Historic Park *(see right)*
Museum of History and Industry *(see p.81)*
Best Museums for Science
Burke Museum of Natural History and Culture *(see p.79)*
Pacific Science Center *(See Children, p.35)*

Left: the Experience Music Project's metallic facade.

irreverent journey through Seattle's history. 'Henry Yesler had no moral or ethical values whatsoever,' one guide announced. 'Naturally he became our first mayor.'

Klondike Gold Rush National Historic Park
319 2nd Avenue S, Pioneer Square; tel: 206-220-4240; www.nps.gov/klgse; daily 9am–5pm; free; bus: 25, 41, 194; map p.134 B3

Learn all about the boom and bust days of the Klondike Gold Rush of 1897–8 in Alaska's Yukon at this indoor museum-like exhibition. Established by the National Parks Service, it preserves the fascinating history of that mining heyday and Seattle's important role as the last stop for provisions before prospectors set out with their dreams of striking it rich. Some of them did – there are success stories, but a great many did not.

Left: visit hidden Seattle on Bill Speidel's Underground Tour.

Several museums have extended hours and offer free admission on the first Thursday of the month (special exhibitions excluded).

continues as an inspection of the shops and rooms that were abandoned when the Pioneer Square area was rebuilt and the levels raised after the Great Fire of 1889. The remaining subterranean city was sealed off until Bill Speidel, an enterprising newspaper columnist, began the conducted tours through the warren of musty, debris-lined passageways and rooms. Passing under the glass-paneled sidewalk at 1st and Yesler, the tour ends at the **Rogues' Gallery**, where old photos, magazines, artifacts, and scale models depict the area as it was before the fire, when Yesler Way was three times as steep as it is today.

Some of the guides in charge of the Underground Tour provide a refreshingly

Seattle Center and Lower Queen Anne

Experience Music Project/ Science Fiction Museum
325 5th Avenue N, Seattle Center; tel: 206-367-5483 for EMP, 206-724-3428 for SFM;

Left: the EMP's fascinating building.

www.empsfm.org; daily 10am–5pm (until 7pm summer); admission charge (free 1st Thur of month 5–8pm); bus: 5, 16, 24, monorail; map p.130 B2
Microsoft co-founder Paul Allen brought the artistic eye of California-based architect Frank Gehry to Seattle Center with the **Experience Music Project**. No one can ignore the structure clad in psychedelic shades of aluminum and stainless steel. The rock 'n' roll building houses an interactive music museum that combines state-of-the-art technology with a world-class collection of artifacts from Jimi Hendrix, Nirvana, KISS, Usher, and many more. For music fans, it's easy to spend hours here looking around.

For something out of this world, visit the spooky **Science Fiction Museum**, the first museum dedicated to the genre. It's situated in a part of the Experience Museum Project building, but its separate entrance and outer walls are electric blue, unlike the dazzling red, purple, and silver of the music museum.

Like the EMP, the SFM houses a collection compiled by Paul Allen. Here, the focus is on sci-fi memorabilia, with pieces on loan from private collections and movie studios. The museum covers everything from novels (gigantic stacks of handwritten pages from one author) to television series (Captain Kirk's chair from *Star Trek*) to blockbuster movies (the alien queen prop from *Aliens*). The Hall of Fame showcases

Right: the Seattle Asian Art Museum on Capitol Hill.

authors and artists whose contributions have shaped the weird and wonderful world of science fiction.
SEE ALSO ARCHITECTURE, P.27

Capitol Hill

Seattle Asian Art Museum
1400 E. Prospect Street, Capitol Hill; tel: 206-654-3100; www.seattleartmuseum.org/visit/visitSAAM.asp; Tue–Wed, Fri–Sun 10am–5pm, Thur 10am–9pm; admission charge (free 1st Thur of month); bus: 10
The imposing Art Deco building in leafy **Volunteer Park** was the original home of the Seattle Art Museum (see p.76), until it outgrew the space. Now it houses an impressive collection of Asian art, including calligraphy, jade sculptures, porcelain, furniture, miniatures, musical instruments, and textiles.
SEE ALSO PARKS, GARDENS, AND BEACHES P.98

Ballard

Nordic Heritage Museum
3014 NW 67th Street, Ballard; tel: 206-789-5707; www.nordicmuseum.org; Tue–Sat 10am–4pm, Sun noon–4pm; admission charge; bus: 17
This Ballard museum provides a background to the story of Scandinavian immi-

> On Sunday early afternoons the **Center for Wooden Boats** (see below) offers free public sails – get there early to sign up, and then enjoy visiting the museum until it's time to cast off!

grants to America. **'The Dream of America'** on the first floor takes visitors back to the journey many made from the old country to America in the 19th century. **'The Promise of America'** on the second floor concentrates on two key industries in which the new immigrants labored: logging and fishing. The third floor focuses on the cultures of each of the different Nordic countries (Denmark, Finland, Iceland, Norway, and Sweden) and the contributions their people made to the Pacific Northwest.

Other Great Neighborhoods

Burke Museum of Natural History and Culture
Corner of 17th Avenue NE and NE 45th Street, University District; tel: 206-543-5590; www.washington.edu/burke museum; daily 10am–5pm (1st Thur of month until 8pm); admission charge (free 1st Thur of month); bus: 25, 49, 70

The Burke Museum celebrates both the natural world and the cultures of the Pacific Rim. Upstairs is a selection of the museum's enormous collection of plant and animal fossils, dinosaur bones, and a large array of creepy-crawlies, butterflies, and moths. There are also rocks and minerals and displays on the evolution of the area's geology – beginning 545 million years ago.

Downstairs the focus is on the culture of indigenous peoples from all around the Pacific Rim, from the Pacific Northwest to Hawaii, Fiji, Korea, Japan, and many other nations. On display are musical instruments, traditional clothing and masks, textiles and utensils, art, and religious artifacts. The videos offer insight into the cultures as they are today.

Center for Wooden Boats
1010 Valley Street, South Lake Union; tel: 206-382-2628; www.cwb.org; daily 10am–6pm, summer: daily 10am–8pm, winter: Tue–Sun 10am–5pm; free (donations welcome): bus: 26, 70, South Lake Union Streetcar
This floating maritime gem keeps alive the tradition of wooden boats on Lake Union. The area was

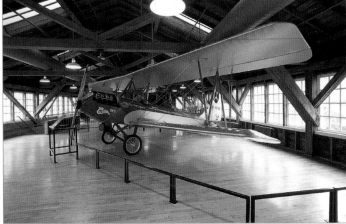

originally a landing site for native Americans who came here to trade goods, and as you walk through the pavilion before reaching the docks, look up to see the traditional carved cedar canoes – a tradition kept alive by the CWB's resident Haida carver. Over time, Lake Union became an important center for the construction of wooden boats, and at its height there were around a dozen shipbuilding yards around the lake. As you walk along the docks, you can see

For a different kind of art experience, join in one of the neighborhood evening art walks, where small galleries and studios open their doors to the public and you can talk directly to the artists. It's a great way to get to know a neighborhood better, to mingle with the locals, and maybe to discover a find from the next great artist. **Pioneer Square** (1st Thursday of month), **Fremont** (1st Friday), **Georgetown** (2nd Saturday), **Ballard** (2nd Saturday), **U-District** (3rd Friday).

a selection of wooden boats, many of which were built in the Lake Union boatyards. The CWB runs a boat shop, where the boats are restored, and there's a visitor center with historic photos. If you want to let the wind fill your sail, a fleet of small craft is available for rental to experienced sailors.

SEE ALSO OUTDOOR ACTIVITIES, P.88

Frye Art Museum

704 Terry Avenue, First Hill; tel: 206-622-9250; www.frye museum.org; Tue–Sat 10am–5pm, Sun noon–5pm; free; bus: 3, 4, 12

The basis of the permanent collection of Charles and Emma Frye, a Seattle couple of German descent whose wealth was made in the meat-packing business, is the work of Munich artists from the late 19th century and early 20th century. In their will the Fryes provided for the establishment of a free museum to display their sizeable art collection. To this day the museum is free, and also hosts gallery talks, films, concerts, and special exhibitions. There is a pleasant Gallery Café for food and beverages.

Henry Art Gallery

Corner of 15th Avenue NE and NE 41st Street, University District; tel: 206-221-4980; www.henryart.org; Tue–Wed, Fri–Sun 11am–5pm, Thur 11am–8pm; admission charge; bus: 25, 49, 70

This gallery on the UW campus exhibits contemporary art from the mid-19th century to the present. Included in its permanent collection are paintings, photography, woodblocks, and textiles, but it has a good reputation for bringing touring exhibitions of modern art to the city, covering all different media from painting and photography to video, film, and sculpture.

Museum of Flight

9404 East Marginal Way S, south of Georgetown; tel: 206-764-5720; www.museumof flight.org; daily 10am–5pm; admission charge (free 1st Thur evening of the month: 5–9pm); bus: 174

This superb museum at Boeing Field is a must-see

Right: old shopfronts at the Museum of History and Industry.

Left: the Museum of Flight.

for visitors to Seattle. In 1916 Bill Boeing flew his first airplane from the banks of Lake Union. Boeing has come a long way since then, but you can still visit the original manufacturing plant, called the Red Barn, which forms part of this amazing museum and documents the pioneering days of air travel.

The six-story **Great Gallery** contains 43 airplanes, including an early 1900 Wright Brothers' model, fighter jets, and ultra-light gliders hanging from the glass ceiling. There are also flight simulators for visitors wanting an extra thrill! The outdoor **Airpark** has more planes, including supersonic Concorde and presidential Air Force One, both of which you can climb aboard if you get there early enough (daily 11am–3.30pm or 4.30pm in summer). **J. Elroy McCaw Personal Courage Wing** focuses on the history of flight during the two World Wars.

Museum of History and Industry

2700 24th Avenue E in McCurdy Park, University District; tel: 206-324-1126; www.seattlehistory.org; daily 10am–5pm (first Thur of month until 8pm); admission charge (free 1st Thur of month); bus: 25, 43, 48

MOHAI offers a fascinating insight into the history of Seattle and the Puget Sound region, from native settlement to the early pioneer days after Captain George Vancouver's ship plied the waters of the Sound in 1792 to the great fire of Seattle in 1889 and the boomtown days of the 1890s. There are reconstructions of early commercial establishments that would have served the gold prospectors, sailors, fishermen, loggers, and all the other citizens who arrived in the new city. Other displays cover the development of the industries upon which the city was built – logging, fishing, mining, the railroads. More recent historical events are covered, too, such as the effect of World War II on the region, and more recently still the booming hi-tech industry led by Microsoft.

Northwest African American Museum (NAAM)

2300 S. Massachusetts Street, Central District; tel: 206-518-

Kids and adults alike will love the **Pacific Science Center**, a dynamic, educational, and fun science museum at the Seattle Center. *See also Children, p.35.*

6000; www.naamnw.org; Wed, Fri 11am–4.30pm, Thur 11am–7pm, Sat 11am–4pm, Sun noon–4pm; admission charge; bus: 7, 42, 48

Opened in 2008 in the former Colman School building, the Northwest African American Museum focuses on the experiences of African Americans in Seattle and the Pacific Northwest. The exhibits are divided into three main sections. The **Journey Gallery** documents the arrival of African Americans, from freed slaves to movement within the United States to more recent arrivals of immigrants from Ethiopia, Sudan, and Somalia in particular. The **Northwest Gallery** showcases local civic and community leaders past and present. The third gallery holds performances, lectures, and other events linked to the main exhibitions.

Music

Seattle is perpetually defined by its music scene. From the highly regarded Seattle Symphony and Seattle Opera to concert series featuring star-studded line-ups and small venues hosting up-and-coming jazz, hip-hop, or indie bands, the city is a mecca for all musical tastes. Long known as the birthplace of grunge rock (à la Kurt Cobain and Eddie Vedder), Seattle's lively music scene has evolved beyond bass guitars and gritty vocals, and is home to a multitude of amazing, diverse bands. There's cross-pollination across genres, with local musicians influencing and shaping the new Seattle sound.

Classical Music and Opera

Seattle Chamber Players
Tel: 206-286-5052; www.seattle chamberplayers.org
The innovative Seattle Chamber Players perform cutting-edge contemporary chamber music at different venues around town.

Seattle Opera
Marion Oliver McCaw Hall, Seattle Center; tel: 206-389-7676; www.seattleopera.org; bus: 3, 4; map p.130 B3
Marion Oliver McCaw Hall is home to the Seattle Opera, directed by Speight Jenkins, with a commonly sold-out year-round schedule and the critically acclaimed Wagner's Ring Cycle performance every four years.

Seattle Symphony
Benaroya Hall, 200 University Street, Downtown; tel: 206-215-4747; www.seattlesymphony.org; bus: 1, 2, 16; map p.133 D2
Classical music aficionados head to Benaroya Hall, where Gerard Schwartz conducts the Seattle Symphony, which celebrated its centennial year in 2003, and a distinguished roster of guest artists perform.

Jazz

Dimitrou's Jazz Alley
2033 6th Avenue, Downtown; tel: 206-441-9729; www.jazz alley.com; Tue–Sun 5.30pm onwards; bus: 70; map p.133 C4
Jazz has a long tradition in Seattle, from the days of Prohibition when the music was underground to the late 1940s when jazz clubs sprang up by the dozen. Duke Ellington, Charlie Parker, and Lester Young all played Seattle, and the local scene boosted the early careers of Quincy Jones, Ray Charles, and Ernestine Anderson. Today that tradition continues at this world-class venue, which has attracted the best jazz, blues, and swing musicians since 1979. Reservations are recommended, for both dinner (Northwest cuisine) and non-dinner tables.

Tula's
2214 2nd Avenue, Belltown; tel: 206-443-4221; www.tulas.com; Sun–Thur 3pm–midnight,

Right: Benaroya Hotel, home to the Seattle Symphony.

Left: the Fleet Foxes are just one of the many great bands to have come out of Seattle.

On the mellower, more melodic side are artists like Sera Cahoone, the Grand Archives, and the Fleet Foxes, with softer, folk-influenced sounds. Hip-hop groups Cancer Rising, Blue Scholars, the Saturday Knights, D. Black, and Scribes are all making a splash, with a soulful and meditative sound. Then there are the fun and wilder electronica/dance bands like Natalie Portman's Shaved Head and Team Gina.

Local labels Sub Pop, Barsuk, Light in the Attic, and Mass Line continue to sign local talent, but there's also a growing scene in DIY, with artists recording their own songs and starting their own labels to release their music, like the Control Group.

Live Music Venues and Clubs

Central Saloon
207 1st Avenue S, Pioneer Square; tel: 206-622-0209; www.centralsaloon.com; daily 11.30am–2am; bus: 21, 22; map p.134 B3
local rock acts are on stage here seven nights a week.

In summer, outdoor concerts feature a top-notch list of popular artists – plus opportunities to enjoy live music while picnicking. The **Woodland Park Zoo** hosts **Zoo Tunes**, drawing artists such as the Indigo Girls and Emmylou Harris. *See also Children, p.34.*

Fri–Sat 3pm–1am; bus: 1, 2, 3; map p.132 C3
Local and regional jazz performers are showcased at Tula's, with occasional visits by some of the heavy-hitters in the jazz world.

Pop, Rock, Hip-Hop, and the Seattle Sound

Throughout the history of the city there have been many influential musicians, from iconic Jimi Hendrix to rapper Sir Mixalot. But Seattle made music history after local music label Sub Pop signed Nirvana in 1988, launching the so-called Seattle Sound. During the grunge era, led by Nirvana, Pearl Jam,

Soundgarden, Mudhoney, and Alice in Chains, Seattle had a very specific sound of simple songs and angst-filled lyrics that others tried to emulate. In the early '90s everyone knew the Seattle Sound, but even then that wasn't the only music coming out of Seattle. Even while grunge was broadcast out to the world, there was a huge pop and indie scene here.

Nowadays there's no specific Seattle Sound per se, but rather lots of different scenes, from soft folk rock to electronica, indie to hip-hop.

Right: the Dave Holland Quintet at Dimitrou's Jazz Alley.

Right: Seattle-based Man Plus performing at Capitol Hill's Comet Tavern.

Chop Suey
1325 E. Madison Street, Capitol Hill; tel: 206-324-8000; www.chopsuey.com; daily 9pm–2am; bus: 2, 10, 11
Chinese-themed Chop Suey books local and national indie, dance, and hip-hop groups.

Comet Tavern
922 E. Pike Street, Capitol Hill; tel: 206-323-9853; daily noon–2am; bus: 10, 11, 49
Capitol Hill's favorite dive bar, with music from live rock bands blaring out Thursday to Saturday (you can catch a pretty good concert without even venturing in), dark-clothed patrons lurking out front, and plenty of beer.

Conor Byrne Pub
5140 Ballard Avenue NW, Ballard; tel: 206-784-3640; www.conor byrnepub.com; daily 3pm–2am; bus: 46, 48
With Guinness and Harp on tap, this Irish pub offers live music most nights of the week, including Celtic, folk, rockabilly, blues, and its old-time social. The bare brick walls and wonderful old lamps hanging from the high ceiling lend an attractive atmosphere.

High Dive
513 N. 36th Street, Fremont; tel: 206-632-0212; www.high diveseattle.com; Mon–Thur 6pm–2am, Fri–Sat 5pm–2am; bus: 28
Full bar, inexpensive food, and live music (indie, alternative, country) or DJs seven nights a week make this a popular local venue.

Nectar Lounge
412 N. 36th Street, Fremont; tel: 206-632-2020; www.nectar lounge.com; daily 4pm–2am; bus: 28

Popular Fremont club with an outdoor terrace, and live music from hip-hop to indie, funk, punk, and soul.

Neumo's
925 E. Pike Street, Capitol Hill; tel: 206-709-9467; www.neumos. com; hours vary, from 8–9pm onwards; bus: 9, 49, 60
Big acts, both local, national, and occasionally international, in a small venue.

Showbox at the Market
1426 1st Avenue, Downtown; tel: 206-628-3151; www.show boxonline.com; hours vary, from

Every Labor Day weekend **Bumbershoot**, one of the nation's largest urban arts festivals, floods the Seattle Center with writers, poets, craftspeople and performing artists. Though music is a primary draw, the non-stop showcase of musicians and rising stars in 30 different indoor and outdoor venues is complemented by crafts booths, fare from local restaurants, and even an animated short-film festival. In typical Seattle fashion, the shows go on, rain or shine. *See also Festivals, p.53.*

7–9pm onwards on show nights; bus: 10, 12, 15; map p.136 A3
A historic ballroom, and one of the city's most illustrious for live music, continually hosting a stellar line-up.

Showbox SoDo
1700 1st Avenue S, SoDo; tel: 206-382-7877; www.showbox online.com; hours vary, from 7–9pm onwards on show nights; bus: 21, 22; map p.134 B1
South of Pioneer Square, this is the even bigger sister space to the original Showbox at the Market *(see left)*.

Sunset Tavern
5433 Ballard Avenue NW, Ballard; tel: 206-784-4880; www.sunsettavern.com; Mon–Sat 6pm–2am, Sun 4pm–2am; bus: 44, 46
A real Ballard institution, the red-themed Sunset Tavern draws live bands most nights of the week, and even offers late-night movies in summer.

ToST
513 N. 36th Street, Fremont; tel: 206-547-0240; www.tostlounge. com; daily 5pm–2am; bus: 28
Live music seven nights a week, with local talent.

Tractor Tavern

5213 Ballard Avenue NW, Ballard; tel: 206-789-3599; www.tractortavern; daily 9.30pm–2am; bus: 44, 46

Draws in country and rockabilly bands and appreciative crowds. Decorated with cowboy boots, tractor tires, and a steer's skull, this medium-sized venue is a great place to see a band.

Music Stores

Bop Street Records

5219 Ballard Avenue NW, Ballard; tel: 206-297-2232; www.bopstreetrecords.com;

Mon–Thur noon–6pm, Fri–Sat noon–midnight, Sun 1–6pm; bus: 44, 46

This warehouse-style store has an astonishing amount of vinyl, with knowledgeable staff, and shows on the weekend.

Easy Street Records

4559 California Avenue SW, West Seattle; tel: 206-938-3279; www.easystreetonline.com; Mon–Sat 9am–9pm, Sun 9am–7pm; bus: 55, 85

Super-cool yet down-to-earth music store with a wide selection of CD and vinyl. There's also a café (serving food 9am–3pm, and beverages 3–8pm daily), and in-store promotions and concerts. (Also at: 20 E. Mercer Street, Lower Queen Anne; tel: 206-691-3279.)

Silver Platters

701 5th Avenue N, Queen Anne; tel: 206-283-3472; www.silverplatters.com; daily 10am–10pm; bus: 3, 16, monorail; map p.130 B3

This CD emporium on Queen Anne also stocks vinyl and some movies.

Left: the Tractor Tavern should please all Rockabilly fans.

Sonic Boom

2209 NW Market Street, Ballard; tel: 206-297-2666; www.sonicboomrecords.com; Mon–Sat 10am–10pm, Sun 10am–7pm; bus: 44, 46

Specializing in independent music, Sonic Boom sells both new and used CDs and vinyl, and has a good offering of local music. They promote in-store performances for local bands and new releases late Monday nights.

(Also at 514 15th Avenue E, Capitol Hill, tel: 206-568-2666.)

The most complete gig listings and music reviews are found in the two free weeklies, *The Stranger* and *Seattle Weekly*. Local radio stations also cover upcoming events: KEXP (90.3FM) for cutting-edge contemporary music, KING (98.1FM) for classical, and KUOW (94.9FM) for general cultural events. Friday's editions of the *Seattle Post-Intelligencer* and *The Seattle Times* contain useful guides to weekend events.

Outdoor Activities

Being out in nature is a way of life for Seattleites, who are as likely to head off to the hills for an after-work hike as they are to be hitting the bars for happy hour. Lakes, forests, and mountains are within reach for boating, hiking, and skiing, marking the Puget Sound region as one of the best locations for outdoor activities in the United States. But you don't even need to leave the city to enjoy the great outdoors, because Seattle has over 400 parks, in-city bike and jogging trails, and golf courses. *See also Parks, Gardens, and Beaches, p.94–9.*

Cycling

Despite its many steep hills, cycling is popular in the Emerald City. In fact, the **Seattle Bicycle Master Plan** is aiming to make Seattle the best community for cycling in the country by 2017. To this end, up to 200 miles (322km) of roadways have bike lane designations added to them to support cycling while making city transportation more eco-friendly and socially sustainable.

But in the meantime, there are several paved trails already in existence. The best-known is the **Burke-Gilman Trail**, which follows the route of an abandoned railroad bed from Ballard's Golden Gardens along the Lake Washington Ship Canal and the University of Washington to Seattle's north city limits at NE 145th Street. The 15-mile (24km) trail follows Lake Washington down by the University. At its northern end it connects with the **Sammamish River Trail**, which follows the Sammamish River from Bothel through Woodinville farmland and ends at Marymoor Park at the north tip of Sammamish Lake. This trail runs for 9½ miles (15km).

Another much shorter route circles **Green Lake** for 3 miles (4.5km); you can circle around as many times as you like, but watch out for the in-line skaters and pedestrians.

West Seattle's **Alki Trail** hugs the waterfront, starting

Left: kayaking on Puget Sound.

Bicycle and Pedestrian Program (tel: 206-684-7583; www.seattle.gov/transportation/bikeprogram.htm). SEE ALSO PARKS, GARDENS, AND BEACHES, P.94–9

BIKE RENTALS AND INFORMATION
Cascade Bicycle Club
Tel: 206-522-BIKE/2453; www.cascade.org
A large bike club that provides information about cycling events in the region.
Gregg's Greenlake Cycle
7007 Woodlawn Avenue NE, Greenlake; tel: 206-523-1822; www.greggscycles.com; Mon–Fri 10am–8pm, Sat–Sun 10am–6pm; bus: 16, 26, 48
Good service, well-established bike rentals.
I 5 Colonnade Park
Beneath Interstate 5, south of E. Howe Street, Capitol Hill; daily 4am–11.30pm; bus: 25
Recycled Cycles
1007 NE Boat Street, U-District; tel: 206-547-4491; www.recycledcycles.com; Mon–Fri 10am–8pm, Sat–Sun 10am–6pm; bus: 70, 72, 73
Good place to rent bikes in the U-District.

at Seacrest Marina and continuing past Alki Beach, at which point it joins the quiet road and continues as far as Lincoln Park. It's 8 miles (13km) one way, and a scenic route if ever there was one. The stretch along Alki Beach gets very busy.

For relaxed weekend riding with fine views of Lake Washington and the Cascade Mountains to the east, a 6-mile (9.5km) stretch of **Lake Washington Boulevard** is closed to cars from the Washington Park Arboretum to Seward Park every third Sunday and second Saturday of the month from May through September.

Mountain bikers can practice their skills at the **I 5 Colonnade Park**, a challenging small course on a steep slope that switches back and forth under the columns supporting the interstate freeway above.

The law requires cyclists to wear a helmet in Seattle

The **STP** – Seattle to Portland Bicycle Classic – is one of the biggest recreational bike rides in the US. Organized by the Cascade Bicycle Club, the 202-mile (325km) ride takes place in July, and brings out thousands of riders who make the journey in two days (a few even manage it in one day).

and King County. More information and a map of biking routes are available from the **City of Seattle's**

Left: the Burke-Gilman Trail.
Right: preparing to ride across the city.

Boating

Bordered by beautiful Puget Sound to the west and fresh-water Lake Washington to the east, Seattle is firmly charted on nautical maps. Opening day of boating season (early May) brings out pleasure boats by the hundreds, but on any weekend or warm evening the Sound and lakes are plied by sailboats, powerboats, kayaks, and canoes. At dawn you can seem teams of rowers on the waters, and at dusk the sailboats paint a pretty picture. Tuesday night is the **Duck Dodge** – a fun-spirited regatta on Lake Union. There are abundant opportunities to get out on the water, even in a rowboat or paddleboat at Green Lake. The water is very accessible and very inviting, but it's also very cold and conditions can change suddenly, so it's important to wear a lifejacket.

BOAT RENTALS AND CLASSES

Agua Verde Café and Paddle Club
1303 NE Boat Street, U-District; tel: 206-545-8570; www.aguaverde.com; daily 10am–6pm (later in summer); bus: 48, 49, 73

Rent a kayak or canoe to take onto Lake Washington, and when you bring it back, stop for a Mexican dinner and a margarita.

Alki Kayak Tours
Seacrest Marina, 1660 Harbor Avenue SW, West Seattle; tel: 206-935-0237; www.kayakalki.com; call or email to make a reservation; bus: 37, 53

Based at Seacrest Park, Alki Kayak Tours rents sea kayaks to experienced kayakers, or beginners can go on a guided kayak tour on Puget Sound, from where you'll get spectacular views of Downtown and the Olympic Mountains. They also rent bikes and in-line skates.

Center for Wooden Boats
1010 Valley Street, South Lake Union; tel: 206-382-2628; www.cwb.org; daily 10am–5pm (until 8pm in summer/closed Mon in winter); bus: 26, 70, South Lake Union Streetcar; map p.131 D3

Experienced sailors can rent the boats from the livery of wooden to sail on Lake Union. There are also a few rowboats, and the CWB runs an excellent program of classes.
SEE ALSO MUSEUMS AND GALLERIES, P.79–80

Green Lake Boat Rentals
7351 E. Green Lake Drive N, Green Lake; tel: 206-527-0171; www.greenlakeboatrentals.net; Apr–Sept: daily 11am–dusk; bus: 16, 48, 358

Rowboats, sailboats, pedal boats, and kayaks are available here to take out onto the calm waters of Green Lake.

Moss Bay Rowing and Kayaking Center
1001 Fairview Avenue N, South Lake Union; tel: 206-682-2031; www.mossbay.net; daily 8am–dusk; bus: 66, 71, 73; map p.131 E4

You can rent kayaks, sailboats, and rowing shells for all experience levels here.

Northwest Outdoor Center
2100 Westlake Avenue N, Suite 1, Lake Union; tel: 206-281-9694; www.nwoc.com; variable, but core hours are summer 10am–6pm, winter 10am–5pm; bus: 5, 17, 26

Kayak rentals and lessons are available alongside Lake Union.

Golf

The golf courses listed below are open to the public, but it's

Skateboarders descend on the small bowl at **Ballard Commons Park** (5701 22nd Ave. NW, Ballard; bus: 44, 46). There are nearby benches if you'd rather watch than participate.

Left: Seattle's position makes it perfect for sailing holidays.

bus: 22, 54, 55
Eighteen-hole, par 72 men, 74 women.

Walking and Hiking

Within the city limits there are ideal trails for shorter hikes, including those at **Discovery Park** with its wooded ravines, forest, grassy meadows, and beach, **Seward Park** and **Schmitz Preserve Park**, both with trails through the old-growth forest, and the bucolic **Washington Park Arboretum**. The 6-mile (10km) urban **Cheslahud Lake Union Loop**, named after a Duwamish chief whose village was located on the lakeshore, links the six neighborhoods surrounding the lake: Fremont, Wallingford, the U-District, Eastlake, South Lake Union, and Queen Anne. It also links the two major lakeside parks (Lake Union Park and GasWorks Park) with 35 tiny street-end parks and water-ways that line the lake. Inter-pretive signs point out the historic landmarks on the way. The paved **Burke-Gilman Trail**, **Alki Trail**, and

a good idea to make reserva-tions since they're very popu-lar. Hours vary with the season; call ahead to confirm.

Green Lake
5701 W. Green Lake Way N, Green Lake; tel: 206-632-2280; Mar–Oct: 9am–shortly before dusk; bus: 16, 66
Nine-hole, par 27; men and women.

Interbay Golf Center
2501 15th Avenue NW, Interbay; tel: 206-285-2200; www.seattle golf.com; Mon–Sat 6am–11pm, Sun 6am–10pm; bus: 15, 17, 18
Nine-hole, par 28; with the added bonus of heated tee stations.

Jackson Park Municipal
1000 NE 135th Street; North-gate; tel: 206-363-4747; www.seattlegolf.com; summer: daily 5.30am–9pm (shorter hours the rest of the year); bus: 73, 47, 348
Eighteen-hole, par 71 men, 73 women.

Jefferson Park Municipal
4101 Beacon Avenue S; tel: 206-762-4513; www.seattlegolf.com; summer: daily 5.30am–9pm (shorter hours the rest of the year); bus: 36
Eighteen-hole, par 70 men and women.

West Seattle Municipal
4470 35th Avenue SW; West Seattle; tel: 206-935-5187; www.seattlegolf.com; summer: 5.30am–9pm daily (shorter hours the rest of the year);

Right: the Green Lake trail is popular with joggers (and dog-walkers).

Green Lake trail *(see Cycling, p.86)*, are very popular with walkers and joggers.

For longer hikes, the **Cascade** and **Olympic Mountains** (and the foothills leading up to them) are home to hundreds of trails, from easy to extremely difficult. A sturdy pair of shoes, food, drink, and warm clothing in layers is essential, and a camera and binoculars will help you to enjoy the magnificent scenery and wildlife. The best sources for information on the hikes are to be found through guidebooks and maps issued by the **Mountaineers**, the **US Forest Service and US National Parks Service**, and the **Washington Trails Association**.
SEE ALSO PARKS, GARDENS, AND BEACHES, P.94–9

ORGANIZED HIKES AND INFORMATION
Mountain Madness
3018 SW Charlestown Street, West Seattle; tel: 206-937-8389; www.mountainmadness.com
Offers personalized outdoor adventure tours including mountain-biking, fishing,

Right: hikers at Rialto Beach in the Olympic National Park.

mountain-climbing, and hiking.
The Mountaineers
300 3rd Avenue W, Queen Anne; tel: 206-284-6310; www.mountaineers.org
An outdoor recreation club that organizes hiking trips and publishes excellent hiking guides.
Sierra Club/
Cascade Chapter
180 Nickerson Street, Suite 202, Queen Anne; tel: 206-378-0114; www.sierraclub.org/wa
Another good resource for information on hiking and outdoor activities.
US Forest Service/
National Parks Service
Outdoor Recreation
Information Office
222 Yale Avenue N, South Lake Union; tel: 206-285-2200; www.nps.gov/ccso/oric.htm
Here you can find up-to-date information on the National Forests and the National Parks.
Washington Trails
Association
2019 3rd Avenue, Suite 100,

Belltown; tel: 206-625-1367; www.wta.org
Has most information needed on trails in the state.

Skiing, snowboarding, and snowshoeing

With the proximity of the Cascade Mountains to the city, opportunities for skiing, snowboarding, snowshoeing, and sledding are practically on Seattle's doorstep. **The Summit at Snoqualmie** is the nearest center, where

there are runs from beginners to advanced. **Crystal Mountain**, located on the slopes of Mount Rainier, is higher and offers longer runs and truly spectacular views. **Stevens Pass** is another popular destination farther north.

Crystal Mountain Ski Area
Highway 410, 40 miles (75km) east of Enumclaw; tel: 360-663-2265; www.crystalmt.com
Washington's largest ski area, and the site of the 1972 World Cup Championships.

Offers a vertical of 3,100ft (945m) and 50 trails for skill levels from beginner to advanced. Weekend night skiing.

Stevens Pass
Summit at Stevens Pass, 70 miles (110km) NE of Seattle; tel: 206-812-4510; www.stevenspass.com
Thirty-seven ski and snowboard trails and a 1,800-ft (550-m) drop, as well as Nordic trails.

Summit at Snoqualmie
50 miles (80km) east of Seattle on I 90 at the Summit of Snoqualmie Pass; tel: 425-434-7669; www.summit-at-snoqualmie.com
Three linked skiing and snowboarding areas – Summit Central, Summit West, and Summit East – together with Alpental across the freeway offer extensive choices of runs, from beginner to expert. Night skiing is also available. For snowboarders, there's a half pipe and jumps in the Sno Park. There is also a Nordic Center, groomed trails for cross-country or snowshoeing, and a groomed slope for sledding.

On any given day you can see folks fishing from the shores of Green Lake, looking very relaxed in their folding chairs and oblivious to the steady stream of walkers, joggers, cyclists, and parents with strollers and dogs passing them on the trail.

Outdoor Gear

Outdoor Research Company
2203 1st Avenue S, SoDo; tel: 206-971-1496; www.orgear.com; Mon–Fri 10am–7pm, Sat 9am–6pm, Sun 11am–5pm; bus: 21, 22, 56
Located south of Pioneer Square, this outdoor outfitter specializes in equipment and clothing for mountaineering, hiking, and climbing.

REI
222 Yale Avenue N, South Lake Union; tel: 206-223-1944; www.rei.com; Mon–Sat 9am–9pm, Sun 10am–7pm; bus: 25, 66, 70; map p.131 E2
This giant among outdoor outfitters, Seattle-based REI (Recreation Equipment Inc.) can meet all your outdoor needs, from skis to bicycles to high-tech clothing, tents, and guidebooks. Their phenomenal flagship store has an exterior mountain-biking trail and an indoor climbing wall too. Expert materials, expert advice, and they also organize hiking trips.

Second Ascent
5209 Ballard Avenue NW, Ballard; tel: 206-545-8810; www.secondascent.com; Mon–Fri 10am–7pm, Sat–Sun 10am–6pm; bus: 44, 46
There are friendly and helpful staff at this second-hand outdoor outfitter, which also rents gear.

Left: fulfil all your outdoor clothing needs at REI, or try their indoor climbing wall.

Pampering

Indulge yourself for the day or just for an hour at one of Seattle's luxurious spas. Treatments range from manicures, pedicures, and facials to full-body wraps, exfoliations, hot stone treatments, and aromatherapy massages. Some offer tailor-made packages for couples, for pregnant women, and special occasions; all offer a sensory experience that transports you from daily life to a place of blissful relaxation. Or just treat yourself to a little bit of luxury back at your hotel with some fun and fragrant soaps and lotions from one of the stores that sell pampering products, a selection of which are listed below.

Lotions and Potions

Bliss Soaps
619 Broadway E, Capitol Hill; tel: 206-322-7627; www.bliss soap.com; Mon, Wed–Fri 3–10pm, Sat 2–10pm, Sun 3–8pm; bus: 9, 49, 60
Looking and smelling good enough to eat, these all-natural, handmade soaps and bath treats will leave you feeling, and smelling, wonderful. Try the grapefruit and pineapple body butter, chocolate and vanilla cupcake bath bomb, or the refreshing mint soap.

Tacoma and Lynwood both have branches of the fabulous and very reasonably priced women-only **Olympus Day Spa** (Tacoma tel: 253-588-3355, Lynwood tel: 425-697-3000; www.olympusspa.net). The all-Korean-style treatments include being scrubbed with soap and mitts in a large room with lots of beds, and indulging in the nude in the many hot baths and steam rooms. A visit here will leave you feeling like a million bucks, without breaking the bank.

Clover House
900 Lenora Street in 2200 Westlake Plaza, South Lake Union; tel: 206-623-0150; www.clover housegifts.com; Mon–Sat 10am–7pm, Sun 11am–5pm; bus: 8, South Lake Union Streetcar; map p.131 D1
Located above Whole Foods, Clover House offers an eclectic collection of lovely bath and body products, jewelry, handbags, and unusual houseplants. Its indulgent and luxurious products include body scrubs, body butters, bubble baths, and lotions by Dani, Olivina, Bella Beauty and Mistral.

Romanza
2206 NW Market Street, Ballard; 206-706-1764; www.romanza gifts.com; Mon–Sat 10am–7pm, Sun 11am–5pm; bus: 44, 46
This gift store has a good offering of pampering products, from satin nightgowns and robes to scented candles and fragrant soaps, lotions and bath milk, handbags, jewelry, and wine. Be sure to look up to see the original Tiffany lamps hanging from the ceiling.

Spas

Banya 5
217 9th Avenue N, South Lake Union; tel: 206-262-1234; www.banya5.com; Tue 4–11pm, Wed–Sun 10am–11pm; bus: 5, South Lake Union Streetcar; map p.131 C2
Come with your significant other or a friend to this reasonably priced Russian-style bathhouse, with hot tubs, a steam room, and a tearoom. Because it's co-ed, swimsuits are required. Private salt scrubs, body mud wraps, deep tissue or relaxation massages, facials and waxing for men and women are

Left and below left: Seattle's spas offer the chance to unwind after a busy day exploring the area.

This Aveda concept salon, spa, and gallery is furnished with a Northwest feel. Using wonderfully scented Aveda products, men and women can opt for the popular Caribbean Body Wrap, Seaweed Body Masque, Reiki, reflexology, or a range of massage treatments, including the Togetherness Massage for you and your someone special.
(Also at 513 N. 36th St, Fremont; tel: 206-633-1339.)

Ummelina International Day Spa
1525 4th Avenue, Downtown; tel: 206-624-1370; www.ummelina.com; Sun–Thur 10.30am–7pm, Fri–Sat 8.30am–9pm; bus: 10, 11, 14; map p.133 D3
The ultimate in luxury, with calming, stimulating, or healing rituals for the mind, body, and spirit. This chic spa with an emphasis on globally sourced products and materials offers amazing Thai, aromatherapy, and hot stone massages, African foot baths, herbal body treatments for men, and many other tantalizing treatments.

also available. Sundays are family days.

Frenchy's Day Spa
3131 E. Madison Street, Madison Park; tel: 206-325-9582; www.frenchysdayspa.com; Mon 9am–5pm, Tue 9am–8pm, Wed–Sat 9am–6pm, Sun 11am–6pm; bus: 11
See and be seen by the techie millionaire wives at this socialite-like spa that gives great anti-ageing facials, bronzing treatments, hot stone massage, toning wraps, Parisian manicures, and pedicures. A range of fabulous lotions and cosmetics from Chantecaille, Molton Brown, and Crème de la Mer are also available.

Gary Manuel Aveda Institute
1514 10th Avenue, Capitol Hill; tel: 206-329-9933; www.gmaveda.com; Tue–Sat 9am–5pm; bus 10, 11, 49
For budget-conscious patrons in need of a stylish cut and color, a cleansing facial, or a soothing full-body massage, this Seattle beauty school fits the bill. Using wonderful-smelling Aveda products, students work under close supervision of instructors, who check and double-check the skin and hair treatments to ensure a good experience for everyone. Bring a willing spirit and a healthy dose of patience, as treatments may take longer than at other salons.

Habitude
2801 NW Market Street, Ballard; tel: 206-782-2898; www.habitude.com; daily 9am–9pm; bus: 44, 46

Right: both the Gary Manual Aveda Institute and Habitude use Aveda products.

Parks, Gardens, and Beaches

With more than 400 parks throughout the city, Seattle has abundant green space for recreation and relaxation. The parks range from postage-stamp-sized areas dotted around Lake Union to vast tracts of open land at Discovery Park. You'll find old-growth forest in Schmitz Preserve Park, attractive beaches at Golden Gardens and Alki, and swimming areas at Seward Park and Green Lake. Seattle's cultivated gardens include Woodland Park and the Japanese Gardens in the Arboretum. *See also Outdoor Activities, p.86–91.*

Alki Beach Park

1702 Alki Avenue SW; West Seattle; tel: 206-684-4075; www.seattle.gov/parks/park spaces/index.htm; mid-Apr–Sept: daily 6am–11pm, Oct–mid-Apr: daily 4am–11.30pm; free; bus: 37, 53

With its unparalleled views of Downtown, Puget Sound, and the majestic Olympic Mountains, Alki attracts the crowds, especially in summer. A 2½-mile (4-km) paved path hugs Elliott Bay from Alki Point (site of the original settlement of Seattle) to Duwamish Head, a magnet for walkers, joggers, skaters, and cyclists. While the water is a little cold for swimming, the sandy beach is great for

A very moving and beautiful sight is the annual tribute to the victims of the atomic bombs that fell on Hiroshima and Nagasaki in World War II. On **August 6** the community gathers on the shores of Green Lake to launch hundreds of wood-and-paper floating lanterns in remembrance of them.

volleyball, barbecues, and picnics.

Carl S. English, Jr, Botanical Gardens

3015 NW 54th Street, Ballard; tel: 206-783-7059; daily 7am–9pm; free; bus: 17, 44

Shortly after the Hiram M. Chittenden Locks *(see p.17)* opened in 1917, a member of the US Army Corps of Engineers, Carl English, designed and then for many years tended this English-style garden on the grounds of the Locks. With over 500 species of plants and flowers, it's a lovely place to explore and to

have a picnic on the hillside overlooking the Locks.

Discovery Park

3801 W. Government Way, Magnolia; tel: 206-386-4236; www.seattle.gov/parks/park spaces/index.htm; daily 6am–11pm; free; bus: 24, 33

This huge, 534-acre (214-hectare) park on Magnolia bluff occupies a spectacular site overlooking the Puget Sound and the Olympic Mountains to the west and the Cascade Mountains to the east. It was once home to the US Army's Fort Lawton, but these days the inhabitants are

Left: the Olympic Sculpture Park and Puget Sound.

hulk of equipment: until the 1950s the site was home to a power plant used to manufacture gas from coal. Two of the old buildings still stand – one is now a picnic shelter, and the other is a children's play barn that preserves the machinery. You can walk the path around and up the hill to the sundial at the top. There are not only lovely views, but also excellent kite-flying conditions. Park facilities include picnic tables and fire grills. The park lies along the route of the Burke-Gilman Trail *(see p.86)*.

Golden Gardens

8498 Seaview Place NW, Ballard; tel: 206-684-4075; www.seattle.gov/parks/park spaces/index.htm; daily 6am–11.30pm; free; bus: 17, 48
This Ballard waterfront park and beach has some of the most sensational water and mountain views in town, plus one of the best beaches. The water is cold for swimming, no matter what time of year, but it's popular with windsurfers and kitesurfers. There's a hand-carry boat launch, too.

Left: sandy Alki Beach.

a rich host of wildlife. It's not uncommon to see bald eagles and hawks soaring above. The upper meadow lands are popular for kite-flying, while the protected 2-mile (3.2km) long tidal beach below is good for sand-combing, wandering to the lighthouse, or watching the ships go by. The park is criss-crossed by wooded hiking trails that connect the different parts. In the northeast section of the park is **Daybreak Star Cultural Center**, a center of Native American culture (www.united indians.org/daybreak.html).

GasWorks Park

2101 N. Northlake Way, Fremont; tel: 206-684-4075; www.seattle.gov/parks/park spaces/index.htm; daily 4am–11.30pm; free; bus: 26
This compact 20-acre (8-hectare) park at the north end of Lake Union offers great views of Downtown and all

If you're in Seattle on New Year's Day, do what the heartier locals do and take the **Polar Bear Plunge** into the icy waters of Lake Washington at Matthews Beach (9300 51st Avenue NE). If you're not feeling so hale and hearty, don a wig instead for the **Old Track Suit Walk** at Green Lake (starts near the wading pool).

the activity on the lake, from sailboats to kayaks to seaplanes. The park is built around the enormous rusting

Right: a picnic in the shadow of GasWorks Park's rusting industrial equipment.

You can fish from the pier at the south end, or admire the restored wetlands from the little bridge at the north end of the park. There are short hikes through the forest trails in the upper park (on the other side of the railroad tracks).

Come to watch the magnificent sunsets, and as darkness falls, it's magical to see groups of people silhouetted against the glow of the fire pits.

Green Lake

7201 E. Green Lake Drive N, Green Lake; tel: 206-684-4075; www.seattle.gov/parks/park spaces/index.htm; 24 hours a day; free; bus: 16, 48, 358 Green Lake is one of Seattle's top recreational parks. Its 3-mile (4.5km) paved path around the lake is always busy with walkers, runners, cyclists, and skaters getting their exercise, any time of the day and into the evening. There are athletic fields that get plenty of use, too, with facilities for soccer, baseball, basketball, and tennis. In warm weather you can swim in a couple of places; there are lifeguards on duty in summer. Rowboats are available for rent, and fishing off the pier or lakeshore is popular.

Other facilities at this beloved park include an indoor pool, a great kids' playground, a popular wading pool (summer), and grassy fields.
SEE ALSO OUTDOOR ACTIVITIES, P.86, 90

Lake Union Park

860 Terry Avenue N, Lake Union; tel: 206-684-7254;

Left: Olympic Sculpture Park.

and to the west by Elliot Bay. A 1¼-mile (2km) paved bike and pedestrian path runs the length of the park, giving visitors access to lovely views of Puget Sound and all the sailboats, container ships, and cruise ships plying its waters, as well as gorgeous views of the Olympic Mountains beyond.

Olympic Sculpture Park

2901 Western Avenue; tel: 206-654-3100; www.seattleart museum.org/visit/OSP; daily sunrise–sunset; free; bus: 1, 8, 15, 18, 99; map p.130 A1/132 A4

In 2007 the **Seattle Art Museum** (see p.76) opened this public park for displaying sculptures by noteworthy artists (including Alexander Calder, Ellsworth Kelly, Richard Serra) in a stunning outdoor setting. The New York architectural firm of Weiss/Manfredi transformed the once industrial site into a garden where sculptures, unbeatable views, and industrial infrastructure all complement one another.

The plot of land is divided into three separate pieces by existing road and train lines, but a zigzag path connects them through **The Valley** with its evergreen plantings, **The Grove** with aspens and other deciduous plantings, and **The Meadow** with its stunning views of Puget Sound and the Olympic

www.seattle.gov/parks/parkspaces/index.htm; bus: 17, 28, 70, South Lake Union Streetcar

Seattle's newest park is due to be completed in 2010, but in the meantime the first 1½ acres (0.6 hectares) of it is open to the public. Eventually occupying 12 acres (5 hectares) of prime real estate on the south end of Lake Union, the vision of the park is to celebrate the unique history and maritime heritage of the region. There is a restored shoreline for wildlife, model boat-sailing area, and **Historic Ships Wharf** that is home to visiting vessels. **The Armory**, formerly the Naval Reserve Building, is scheduled to become the new home of the Museum of History and Industry in 2012. Two important partners in the park are the **United Indians of All Tribes**, who will build an educational center here, and the adjacent **Center for Wooden Boats**.

SEE ALSO MUSEUMS AND GALLERIES, P.79–80

Left: taking a rest at Green Lake.

Lincoln Park

8011 Fauntleroy Way SW, West Seattle; tel: 206-684-4075; www.seattle.gov/parks/park spaces/index.htm; daily 4am–11.30pm; free; bus: 54

West Seattle's Lincoln Park is a mecca for walkers. A wide, paved waterfront path provides the same magnificent views and invigorating saltwater air as at Alki, but without the crowds. The path leads to **Colman Pool**, an outdoor, heated, saltwater swimming pool (open in summer). Sea kayakers and others with hand-carried boats can take advantage of the boat launch. Hiking trails (5 miles/8km of them) lead into the upper park, which is wooded and peaceful. There are picnic tables, a play area, football, soccer, and baseball facilities.

Myrtle Edwards Park

3130 Alaskan Way W, Lower Queen Anne; tel: 206-684-4075; www.seattle.gov/parks/park spaces/index.htm; 24 hours a day; free; bus: 99; map p.132 A4/130 A1

This long, thin strip of a park north of Pier 70 is bordered to the east by railroad tracks,

Seattle is full of dogs and dog-lovers. Many parks have off-leash areas for your dogs to run around, and some also provide bags for cleaning up your dog's mess. The local citizenry are very conscientious about cleaning up after their dogs; please follow their lead!

If you go for a swim in one of the lakes, it's wise to shower afterwards to avoid the potential and rather uncomfortable 'swimmer's itch'!

Mountains to the west. The path continues to a driftwood beach and tidal garden.

Schmitz Preserve Park

5551 SW Admiral Way, West Seattle; tel: 206-684-4075; www.seattle.gov/parks/park spaces/index.htm; daily 4am–11.30pm; free; bus: 51, 56

It was the foresight of a German immigrant named Schmitz, together with some other landowners around 1908, who donated the land that eventually formed this 50-acre (20-hectare) park. Their efforts to protect the forest land that was rapidly being cleared allow us to enjoy this peaceful and beautiful haven. The moment you enter the old-growth forest the hustle and bustle of the city fade away, to be replaced by a hush that is punctuated only by birdsong.

Seward Park

5898 Lake Washington Blvd S, Seward Park; tel: 206-684-

4396; www.seattle.gov/parks/parkspaces/index.htm; daily 6am–11pm (parking lot closes at 10pm); free; bus: 39

This 300-acre (120-hectare) South Seattle park occupying a promontory into Lake Washington is home to the largest section of old-growth forest in the city. The bulk of the trees are Douglas fir, but there are also lots of maples, madronas, and cedar trees. Extensive hiking trails lead through the forest, and you may be lucky to see bald eagles, woodpeckers, or western screech owls in addition to ducks, herons, and coots. River otters and turtles frequent the park's shores.

Seward Park has a great roped-off swimming area, with a lifeguard in summer. There's also a beach on the south side, a 2½-mile (4-km) bike and walking path, and a native plant garden.

Volunteer Park

1247 15th Avenue E, Capitol Hill; tel: 206-684-4075; www.seattle. gov/parks/parkspaces/ index.htm; daily 6am–11pm; free (donation suggested for Conservatory); bus: 10, 12

Capitol Hill's largest park and home to the **Seattle Asian Art Museum**, Volunteer Park was named in honor of the volunteers of the Spanish-American War (1898–1902). The park was designed by the Olmsted Brothers, who also built the **Water Tower** (1906) near the park's south entrance that rewards those who climb it with impressive views. Other features include a reservoir with a jogging trail around it, a tennis court, and a popular children's playground with a wading pool (filled in sum-

mer). All parts of the park have easy access from the car, making it a great park for picnics on the well-tended lawns.

One of the main attractions is the **Conservatory**, built in 1912. Open daily from 10am–4pm (until 6pm in summer), it is formed of five adjoining 'houses': Bromeliad House, Palm House, Fern House, Seasonal Display House, and Cactus House. The orchid collection is particularly fine, with over 600 varieties.

At night the park has a reputation for being a gay pick-up area.

SEE ALSO MUSEUMS AND GALLERIES, P.79

Washington Park Arboretum

2300 Arboretum Drive E, Montlake; tel: 206-543-8800; http://depts.washington.edu/ wpa/index.htm; daily dawn–dusk; free; bus: 11 43, 48 (McGraw St stop)

Right: Washington Park Arboretum in the fall.

10am–4pm; admission charge; bus: 11, 84

Within the Washington Park Arboretum is this formal Japanese garden designed in 1960 by Juki Iida. The secluded garden provides a peaceful retreat with water features that include koi carp, meandering paths, a traditional teahouse, and thoughtfully planted and gracefully pruned trees and shrubs. The Japanese maples are beautiful, and in spring the cherry blossoms are lovely. Look closely at the water's edge and you may see one of the many turtles that make their home here.

Woodland Park Rose Garden

750 N. 50th, Fremont; tel: 206-233–7272; www.zoo.org/ zoo_info/rosegarden/rose garden.html; daily 4am–11.30pm; free; bus: 5, 44

One of only 24 certified American Rose Test Gardens in the United States, this formal rose garden is a delight to the senses. With over 5,000 plants and 280 varieties of roses, it is at its most impressive between May and August when the roses are in full, glorious bloom.

The Arboretum is known for its amazing tree collection, spread over 230 acres (92 hectares). In spring, you can walk the broad grassy avenue admiring the blossoms, while in fall every photographer in town descends to capture the fiery oranges, reds, and golds of the autumn foliage. Trails lead through the different areas, where you can observe camellias, rhododendrons, Japanese maples, magnolias, walnuts, and many other collections of trees.

JAPANESE GARDEN
1075 Lake Washington Blvd E; tel: 206-684-4725; www.seattle.gov/parks/park spaces/index.htm; Mar, mid-Sept–mid-Oct: Tue–Sun 10am–6pm, Apr: Tue–Sun 10am–7pm, May–mid-Aug: daily 10am–8pm, mid-Aug–mid-Sept: daily 10am–7pm, mid-Oct–Nov: Tue–Sun

Restaurants

The burgeoning Seattle restaurant scene offers quality dining to satisfy all tastes and budgets. There is an increasing focus on quality, local ingredients, especially fish and seafood, naturally raised meat and poultry, and organic produce. In terms of where to eat, Downtown and Belltown have some of the fancier restaurants; Asian restaurants abound in the International District; and Capitol Hill, Fremont, and Ballard are home to decent neighborhood eateries. Columbia City has a number of good restaurants concentrated within a few blocks of each other. *See also Coffee Shops, p.36–41, and Food and Drink, p.56–7.*

Downtown and Belltown

NORTHWEST CUISINE

boka Kitchen + Bar
1010 1st Avenue; tel: 206-357-9000; www.bokaseattle.com; Mon–Fri 11am–10pm, Sat 8am–2pm and 5–10.30pm, Sun 8am–2pm and 5–10pm; $$$; bus: 10, 15, 18; map p.133 D1
Lovely presentation of creative American classics such as salmon, steak, and pastas using the freshest Northwest ingredients. In Seattle's upscale Hotel 1000 *(see p.64)*, also a place to see and be seen.

Dahlia Lounge
2001 4th Avenue, Belltown; tel: 206-682-4142; www.tomdouglas.com; Mon–Fri 11.30am–2.30pm and 5–10pm (Fri until 11pm), Sat 5–11pm, Sun 5–10pm; $$$$; bus: 13, 16; map p.133 C2

Prices for a three-course dinner per person with half a bottle of wine:
$ = under $20
$$ = $20–45
$$$ = $45–60
$$$$ = more than $60

One of the earlier Tom Douglas restaurants on the Seattle scene, Dahlia Lounge is known for a short but innovative Northwest menu featuring fresh seafood such as dungeoness crab, Penn Cove manila clams, shrimp potstickers, grilled and rotisserie meats, and fresh pastries and desserts from the bakery next door.

Matt's in the Market
94 Pike Street, Suite 32; tel: 206-467-7909; www.mattsinthemarket.com; Mon–Sat 11.30am–2.30pm and 5.30–10pm; $$$; bus: 10, 15, 18; map p.136 A3
The tiny second-floor dining room overlooks Pike Place Market, and is one of the best places for watching the bustling scene below. Lunch brings catfish and oyster po'boy sandwiches, and favorite dinner entrées feature fresh fish.

Palace Kitchen
2030 5th Avenue; tel: 206-448-2001; www.tomdouglas.com; daily 5pm–1am; $$$; bus: 13, 26, 28; map p.133 C4
Another Tom Douglas restaurant, this one under the monorail, offers great-value and surprisingly generous appetizers. With its huge horseshoe-shaped bar, the place can get pretty boisterous later in the evening hours, and the kitchen stays open until 1am.

AFRICAN

Pan Africa
1521 1st Avenue; tel: 206-652-2461; Sun–Tue 10am–6pm, Wed–Sat 10am–8pm; $; bus: 10,

Right and above left: the busy kitchen at Matt's in the Market and one of its tasty creations.

Left: the terrace at Ivar's Salmon House *(see p.108)*.

break the scales with their girth, but the service with a flourish really makes this place.

ASIAN
Six Seven
2411 Alaskan Way; tel: 206-269-4575; www.edgewaterhotel.com; Sun–Thur 6.30am–9.30pm, Fri–Sat 6.30am–10pm; $$$–$$$$; bus: 99; map p.132 B3

Dining at Six Seven is like eating in a floating forest lodge. Large tree trunks serve as architectural support, while the floor-to-ceiling windows display views of Elliott Bay and the Olympic Mountains. Upscale pan-Asian and American cuisine.

Wild Ginger
Asian Restaurant
1401 3rd Avenue; tel: 206-623-4450; www.wildginger.net; Mon–Thur 11.30am–3pm and 5–11pm, Fri 11.30am–3pm and 5pm–midnight, Sat 11.30am–3pm and 4.30pm–midnight, Sun 4pm–11pm; $$$; bus: 1, 2, 3; map p.133 D2

Although the dishes draw inspiration from sources as diverse as Singapore, Bangkok, Saigon, and

---

> Good service warrants a tip of 15–20 percent of the pre-tax amount on the bill.

15, 18; map p.136 C2

Native Ethiopian Mulugeta Abeta opened his Pike Place Market restaurant in 2003. About half of the menu is Ethiopian; the other half changes monthly, with specialties from other African countries. One of the more popular Seattle destinations for vegans.

AMERICAN
Metropolitan Grill
820 2nd Avenue; tel: 206-624-3287; www.themetropolitangrill.com; Mon–Fri 11am–3pm and 5–10.30pm, Sat 4–11pm, Sun 4–10pm; $$$$; bus: 1, 12, 13; map p.134 B4

With the number of awards the Metropolitan has received – including 'Seattle's Best Steakhouse' – you might expect complacency. Not a bit of it. The steaks are done within a degree of your preferred temperature and

Le Pichet
1933 1st Avenue; tel: 206-256-1499; www.lepichetseattle.com; Sun–Thur 8am–midnight, Fri–Sat 8am–2am; $$; bus: 10, 15, 18; map p.136 A2

This cute French café is regularly acclaimed by locals as one of the best French restaurants in town. The fare is simple and delicious, from plates of *charcuterie* or *fromage* to roast chicken or beef, with good espresso and pastries.

ITALIAN
The Pink Door
1919 Post Alley; tel: 206-443-3241; www.thepinkdoor.net; Mon–Thur 11.30am–10pm, Fri 11.30am–11pm, Sun 4–11pm; $$$; bus: 99; map p.136 A2

The lack of signage hasn't kept folks from finding this Pike Place Market favorite. Unpretentious Italian food and regular shows in the adjacent bar, but best of all are the views of Puget Sound from the sheltered deck.

Tulio
1100 5th Avenue; tel: 206-624-5500; www.tulio.com; Mon–Thur 7am–10pm, Fri 7am–11pm, Sat 8am–11pm, Sun 8am–5pm; $$$; bus: 2, 11, 70; map p.133 D2

Located in the Hotel Vintage Park *(see p.65)*, Tulio is more than just a hotel restaurant. Authentically Italian delicacies include house-cured meats, fresh pastas, and baked focaccia. Save enough space for the *gelato*.

SEAFOOD
The Crab Pot
1301 Alaskan Way; tel: 206-624-1890; www.pier57seattle.com/

Jakarta, this restaurant doesn't suffer from any lack of focus. Favorites include the coconut laksa (a Malaysian seafood soup) and the fragrant duck. The mahogany satay bar offers scallops, eggplant, or wild-boar skewers.

FRENCH
Café Campagne
1600 Post Alley; tel: 206-728-2233; www.campagnerestaurant.com; Mon–Thur 11am–10pm, Fri–Sat 8am–11pm, Sun 8am–10pm; $$; bus: 10, 15, 18; map p.136 A2

Prices for a three-course dinner per person with half a bottle of wine:
$ = under $20
$$ = $20–45
$$$ = $45–60
$$$$ = more than $60

The 'little brother' of Campagne restaurant *(see below)*, and in no way inferior to its pricier sibling, just a little less complicated. The quiches are light and fluffy, the salads and soups succulent, the atmosphere very civilized.

Campagne
Inn at the Market, 86 Pike Street; tel: 206-728-2800; www.campagnerestaurant.com; daily 5.30–10pm; $$$$; bus: 10, 15, 18; map p.136 A2

Campagne does the right things right. The service is impeccable, the appetizers – especially the soups – are exquisite, and the wine list is comprehensive without being overwhelming. A wine steward friend confides that their red and white burgundy list is the best in the city. Anyone who appreciates food will enjoy Campagne.

restaurants.html; Sun–Thur 11am–9pm, Fri–Sat 11am–10pm; $$$; bus: 99; map p.133 C1
Centrally located on the waterfront piers, the Crab Pot is a great place for tasty, fresh seafood. In the summer, sit at one of the patio tables and enjoy the fresh breeze from the Sound as you dine.

Etta's Seafood
2020 Western Avenue; tel: 206-443-6000; www.tomdouglas.com; Mon–Thur 11.30am–9.30pm, Fri 11.30am–10pm, Sat 9am–10pm, Sun 9am–9pm; $$$; bus: 15, 18, 21; map p.136 A1
Tom Douglas's restaurant by Pike Place Market is not all seafood, but fish is the highlight. Locally raised poultry and beef are also featured. Don't skimp on the side dishes, either; the servers give excellent advice on what best complements what.

Red Fin
620 Stewart Street; tel: 206-441-4340; www.redfinsushi.com; 6am–1am daily; $$$; bus: 25, 66, 70; map p.133 D3
Sleek and stylish sushi restaurant adjoining the equally stylish Hotel Max (see p.65), with helpful and knowledgeable wait staff. Asian fusion cuisine and a good selection of sakes.

There are few vegetarian restaurants in the city, but many menus include more meat-free dishes on the menu, or the kitchen will prepare something upon request.

Pioneer Square and the International District

AMERICAN
New Orleans Creole Restaurant
114 1st Avenue S; tel: 206-622-2563; http://neworleanscreolerestaurant.com; Mon–Thur 9.30am–10pm, Fri 9.30am–1.30pm, Sat noon–1.30pm; $$; bus: 15, 18; map p.134 B4
In Pioneer Square's historic Lombardy building, this restaurant is the spot for live music and good Louisiana cooking. Local and national musicians play jazz, Dixieland, blues and more as patrons enjoy Creole and Cajun favorites like jambalaya and gumbo.

ASIAN
China Gate
516 7th Avenue S; tel: 206-624-1730; daily 10am–2am; $$; bus: 7, 14, 36; map p.135 D3
Perfect for large gatherings, this airy restaurant with its ornate exterior is dependable for good Chinese food. Free

parking is available weekends.

Jade Garden
424 7th Avenue S; tel: 206-622-8181; Mon–Thur 9am–2.30am, Sat 9am–3.30am, Sun 9am–1am; $$; bus: 7, 14, 36; map p.135 D3
The long line of diners waiting to get in snakes out the door and around the corner. The dim sum is hands down the best in all of Seattle, and the price is decent, too. Regular menu items are also tasty and fresh – seafood is so fresh it's likely swimming in the restaurant's tanks until an order comes in.

Maneki
304 6th Avenue S; tel: 206-622-2631; Tue–Sun 5.30–10pm; $$; bus: 7, 14, 36; map p.135 C3
Locals have long raved about Maneki's divine sushi, as well they might. With over 100 years of service, this is the oldest sushi restaurant in town, and the large menu has reasonably priced treats. Reservations are a good idea, since it's a small and popular place.

Sea Garden
509 7th Avenue S; tel: 206-623-2100; Mon–Thur 11am–2am, Fri–Sat 11am–3am, Sun 11am–1am; $$–$$$; bus: 7, 14, 36; map p.135 D3

This is Seattle Chinese seafood at its best. Some find the flavors are a tad Americanized, but they're close enough to the real deal to draw plenty of Asian diners. Standout dishes include salt and pepper-seasoned deep-fried calamari and crab in black-bean sauce.

Shanghai Garden
524 6th Avenue S; tel: 206-625-1689; Sun–Thur 11am–9.30pm, Fri–Sat 11am–10.30pm; $$; bus: 7, 14, 36; map p.135 C3

This spot offers dishes that are common in China, but are harder to find in the States. Hog's maw and black fungus are among the authentic Chinese offerings. The less adventurous need not shy away; tasty and healthy dishes like the hand-shaven

Prices for a three-course dinner per person with half a bottle of wine:
$ = under $20
$$ = $20–45
$$$ = $45–60
$$$$ = more than $60

barley green noodles and pea vines are also available.

Uwajimaya
600 5th Avenue S; tel: 206-624-6248; www.uwajimaya.com; Mon–Sat 9am–10pm, Sun 9am–9pm; $ bus: 26, 28, 42; map p.134 C2

Kill two birds with one stone at this Asian grocery store – shop for exotic items, then head over to the food court. There, you'll find a variety of Asian fast-food cuisine, ranging from Chinese to Korean to Vietnamese.

SEE ALSO FOOD AND DRINK, P.57

IRISH

Fado Irish Pub
801 1st Avenue; tel: 206-264-2700; www.fadoirishpub.com; daily 11.30am–2am; $; bus: 15, 18, 21; map p.134 B2

A Pioneer Square pub filled with Irish memorabilia. Relax with a 'perfect pint' (a 20-ounce glass shaped to fit the palm) and traditional fare such as shepherd's pie and bangers 'n' mash, as well as American favorites. Irish

bands and dancing are also a draw, but there's no set schedule for these events.

ITALIAN

Il Terrazzo Carmine
411 1st Avenue S; tel: 206-467-7797; www.ilterrazzocarmine.com; Mon–Fri 11.30am–2.30pm and 5.30–10.30pm, Sat 5.30–10.30pm; $$$$; bus: 15, 18, 21; map p.134 B3

This romantic Italian restaurant in a Pioneer Square office building has been a consistent customer-pleaser for more than 20 years, and has a loyal regular clientele. In the light, white-tableclothed dining room, patrons enjoy professional service and classic Italian specialties like *gnocchi Sorrentina*, *cioppino* and *osso bucco*. The alley patio is surprisingly intimate.

Salumi
309 3rd Avenue S; tel: 206-621-8772; www.salumicured

Right: Seattle's love for fresh fish means there are some pretty good sushi restaurants.

Left: buy fresh ingredients at Uwajimaya or eat at its fantastic food court.

meats.com; Tue–Fri 11am–4pm; $; bus: 7, 14, 70; map p.134 C3

Lines at lunchtime are long at this Pioneer Square eatery, and meat-lovers swear by Armandino Batali's house-cured cuts put into mouth-watering sandwiches. The specials change weekly, but include tasty soups and pasta dishes.

Seattle Center and Lower Queen Anne

NORTHWEST CUISINE
Sky City

400 Broad Street; tel: 206-950-2100; www.spaceneedle.com/restaurant; 11am–2.45pm and Mon–Fri 5–10pm, Sat–Sun 9.30am–2.45pm and 5–10pm; $$$$; bus: 3, 14, 16; map p.130 B2

It takes an hour for your seat to rotate around the retro restaurant at the top of the **Space Needle** (see p.26), but you'll want to linger at least that long for the view. Prices are high, but the elevator ride

is free and the cuisine is better than locals claim.

AMERICAN
Mecca Café

526 Queen Anne Avenue N; tel: 206-285-9728; daily 24 hours; $; bus: 1, 13, 15; map p.130 A3

For a true dive bar with great food in Seattle, try the Mecca. It's popular with the late-night crowd for its stiff pours and round-the-clock classic American fare, including burgers and fries. The breakfasts are good for the morning after, too.

ASIAN
Bamboo Garden

364 Roy Street; tel: 206-281-6616; www.bamboogarden.net; daily 11am–10pm; $; bus: 3, 4; map p.130 B3

Though the menu includes familiar dishes such as kun pao chicken, everything is vegetarian; all of the 'meat' is made from vegetable protein – some of which tastes remarkably meaty. Often crowded, but the wait isn't long.

Sushi Land

803 5th Avenue N; tel: 206-267-7621; www.sushilandusa.com;

People here tend to eat early, with breakfast from 7am, lunch from 11am, and dinner from 5pm. Many restaurants have finished the dinner service by 9pm.

daily 11am–9pm; $; bus: 3, 4; map p.130 B3

Sit at the counter and grab what you want as it glides by. This is conveyor-belt sushi at its best – fun, delicious, and cheap. Sure, it's not top-notch sushi, but considering the price, it's darn good. Seasonal specials like Copper River salmon.

FRENCH/SWISS
The Melting Pot

14 Mercer Street; tel: 206-378-1208; www.meltingpot.com; Mon–Thur 5–10pm, Fri 5–10.30pm, Sat 4–10.30pm, Sun 4–10pm; $$$; bus: 1, 13, 15; map p.130 A3

The Melting Pot is fun with fondue. Cozy into a booth with your own tabletop fondue pot, start with cheese, and end with chocolate. Featured entrées include lobster tail and filet mignon, as well

105

as simpler fare like ravioli and chicken. Valet parking is available, with a charge.

MIDDLE EASTERN
Mediterranean Kitchen
366 Roy Street; tel: 206-285-6713; Mon–Sat 11am–9pm, Sun 5–9pm; $$; bus: 3, 4; map p.130 B3

Atmosphere is not what draws people to this restaurant – it's the rich aroma of garlic, and dishes like schwarma, shish tawook and couscous. Platters come with hummus and rice, and as spicy as you want them.

SEAFOOD
Waterfront Seafood Grill
2815 Alaskan Way, Pier 70; tel: 206-956-9171; waterfront

Prices for a three-course dinner per person with half a bottle of wine:
$ = under $20
$$ = $20–45
$$$ = $45–60
$$$$ = more than $60

pier70.com; daily 5–10pm; $$$$; bus: 99; map p.132 A4

On the waterfront side of the Olympic Sculpture Park, the views are the main attraction here, but the well-prepared seafood is a close second. There are also steaks, as well as desserts worth saving room for.

Capitol Hill
NORTHWEST CUISINE
Lark
926 12th Avenue; tel: 206-323-5275; www.larkseattle.com; Tue–Sun 5–10.30pm; $$$–$$$$; bus: 3, 11, 12

Shareable platters, an oft-changing menu, and knowledgeable servers add to the appeal of this charming Capitol Hill bistro. Flickering candlelight and the buzz of the food-savvy beautiful people complement dishes, which range from seared Sonoma foie gras to carpaccio of yellowtail.

Crave
1621 12th Avenue; tel: 206-388-0526; www.cravefood.com;

daily 8am–11pm; $–$$; bus: 8, 11, 43

Crave bills itself as serving 'honest food,' and the menu and friendly service live up to the billing. Food changes by the season with local and foreign dishes, but favorites include curried lamb, goats' cheese gnocchi, and shiitake macaroni and cheese.

AMERICAN
Deluxe Bar & Grill
625 Broadway E; tel: 206-324-9697; daily 11am–2am; $$; bus: 9, 49, 60

Relax with a meal of American classics in this casual restaurant at the north end of Broadway.

A diverse selection of local microbrew beers makes a great complement to the half-price burger specials offered every Wednesday.

Elysian Brewing Co.
1221 E. Pike Street; tel: 206-860-1920; www.elysian brewing.com; Mon–Fri 11.30am–11pm, Sat–Sun noon–2am; $; bus: 11, 12

Left and below: wash down your steak with one of the Elysian Brewing Co's beers.

A wide selection of micro-brew beers is the biggest draw here. Some are brewed on the premises and others imported, and the pub food is not too bad, either, with vegetarian and vegan options as well as hearty meat dishes. You won't leave hungry.

The Kingfish Cafe
602 19th Avenue E; tel: 206-320-8757; www.thekingfish cafe.com; Mon–Thur 11.30am–2pm and 5.30–9pm, Fri 11.30am–2pm and 5.30–10.30pm, Sat 10am–2pm and 5.30–10.30pm, Sun 10am–2pm and 5.30–9pm; $$; bus: 12
Southern soul food, served up with style, sauce, and smiles. The grits go well with everything, and the catfish is pretty miraculous, as is the fried chicken. Long lines attest to the café's popularity, particularly for weekend brunch.

EUROPEAN
B & O
204 Belmont Avenue E; tel: 206-322-5028; Mon–Fri 7am–midnight, Sat 7am–1am,

Sun 9am–midnight; $$; bus: 8, 43
A Capitol Hill institution, this European-style bistro at the corner of Belmont and Olive serves a variety of Mediter-ranean, Middle Eastern, and American dishes in a relaxed setting. Dinner is served until late, and it's also a great spot for coffee and delicious desserts. Breakfast is popular, too.

Café Septième
214 Broadway Avenue E; tel: 206-860-8858; daily 9am–midnight; $$; bus: 9, 49, 60
Capitol Hill cool spot on Broadway. Inexpensive but inventive bistro menu and strong drinks. The staff range from charming to coldly indif-ferent. It's darkly lit with blood-red walls, deep, cozy booths, and a particularly fine selection of desserts.

Dinette
1540 E. Olive Way; tel: 206-328-2282; www.dinetteseattle.com; Tue–Thur 5–9pm, Fri–Sat 5.30–10pm; $$; bus: 14, 43
This delightful small bistro offers rustic European food in a relaxed but elegant setting. There is a tempting selection of toast with different spreads and toppings, bowls of pasta or stew, and flavorful

It's very common and perfectly acceptable to ask for your leftovers to be boxed up to take with you. But as from 2010 the boxes will no longer be made of Styrofoam, since the Seattle City Council recently voted to ban these non-biodegradable containers from city restaurants.

fish and poultry. A little gem of a neighborhood restaurant.

ITALIAN
Via Tribunali
913 E. Pike Street; tel: 206-321-9234; www.viatribunali.com; daily 5pm–2am; $$; bus: 9, 11, 60
Be prepared to wait for a table at this dark, sexy Cap-itol Hill favorite. This sophisti-cated Italian pizzeria has been out-the-door popular since the day it opened. Many ingredients come from Italy, giving the pizzas a taste of authenticity.

SEAFOOD
Coastal Kitchen
429 15th Avenue E; tel: 206-321-1145; www.chowfoods.com; daily 8am–11pm; $$; bus: 10
This hip Capitol Hill hang-out keeps diners guessing with

Brad's Swingside Café
4212 Fremont Avenue N; tel: 206-633-4057; Tue–Sat 5.30–10pm; $$; bus: 82

Walk in the door of this funky Fremont bungalow and you might think you'd walked into a private party in someone's home. Excellent Italian food; start with antipasti, and move on to pastas and specials.

SEAFOOD
Ivar's Salmon House
401 NE Northlake Way; tel: 206-632-0767; www.ivars.net; Mon–Thur 11am–9pm, Fri–Sat 11am–10pm, Sun 9.30am–9pm; $$$; bus: 26

About a mile east of the center of Fremont, totem poles greet you at this seafood restaurant styled after a Native American longhouse with carvings, historic paintings, and artifacts. You can dine in the bar, where happy-hour snacks and drinks are great value, or opt for the more upscale dining room.

Ponti Seafood Grill
3014 3rd Avenue N; tel: 206-284-3000; www.pontigrill.com; daily 5–10pm; $$$; bus: 26

A local favorite for more than 15 years, Ponti serves Northwest seafood in a location overlooking the Lake Washington Ship Canal and the Fremont drawbridge. In warm weather, enjoy the great views and great atmosphere on the patio, especially at happy hour.

its regularly changing menu that features foods from coastal communities around the world. How the cooks do so well at so many different ethnic styles is a mystery, but they do.

Fremont

AMERICAN
Norm's Eatery and Ale House
460 N. 36th Street; tel: 206-547-1417; Mon–Wed 11am–midnight, Thur–Fri 11am–2am, Sat 10am–2am, Sun 10am–midnight; $; bus: 26, 28

Good old American fare of chicken, burgers, and salads

Prices for a three-course dinner per person with half a bottle of wine:
$ = under $20
$$ = $20–45
$$$ = $45–60
$$$$ = more than $60

at this relaxed, dog-friendly establishment popular with the younger crowd. Have a cold beer or try one of the canine-themed drinks (such as Doggie Biscuitini and Woo-Woo). Doggie décor throughout.

ITALIAN
Asteroid
3601 Fremont Avenue N; tel: 206-547-9000; www.asteroid cafe.com; Sun–Mon 5–10pm, Tue–Thur 11.30am–2pm and 5–10pm, Fri 11.30am–2pm and 5–11pm, Sat 5–11pm; $$–$$$; bus: 26, 28

This Italian neighborhood restaurant in the center of Fremont serves spicy *puttanesca*, vegetarian *ravioli ai carciofi* (with artichokes), traditional stew of wild boar, steaks, and wine-by-the-glass specials (lots of Italian wines). Good choice for vegetarians too.

Ballard

AMERICAN
Lockspot Café
3005 NW 54th Street; tel: 206-789-4865; Mon–Fri 11am–

For late-night food, the International District has a number of restaurants serving food until 2 or even 3am. Other options for late-night nibblers are bars, where snacks and sometimes substantial meals are available.

2am, Sat–Sun 8am–2am; $; bus: 44, 46
Right by the entrance to the Hiram A. Chittenden Locks *(see p.17)* is this slightly run-down neighborhood café, great for breakfasts and fish and chips; you can take your food out and have a picnic while watching the boats navigate through the locks. Or hang out and play some pool or pinball.

Old Town Alehouse
5233 Ballard Avenue NW; tel: 206-782-8323; www.oldtownalehouse.com; Sun–Mon 11.30am–10pm, Tue–Thur 11.30am–11pm, Fri–Sat 11.30am–midnight; $$; bus: 44, 46
Offering a good range of seasonal taps, in addition to great fish and chips with seasoned fries and fresh coleslaw, salads, and hefty sandwiches, you can relax in the attractive, airy, and welcoming surroundings here.

The Hi-Life
5425 Ballard Avenue NW; tel: 206-784-7272; www.chowfoods.com; Sun–Thur 8.30am–3pm and 5–10pm, Fri–Sat 8.30am–3pm and 5–11pm; $$; bus: 44, 46
Located in the old Ballard firehouse, this restaurant changes its menu quarterly, but features wood-fired pizzas (with toppings such as wild mushrooms or Italian sausage with fennel), sirloin or porterhouse steaks, and fresh pasta. Generous portions, sophisticated ambience, and a popular bar (especially at happy hour).

hot-from-the-oven pizzas and good pastas, but save room for the 'orgasm' – a giant cookie baked in the pizza oven then topped with ice cream.

Volterra
5411 Ballard Avenue NW; tel: 206-789-5100; www.volterrarestaurant.com; Mon–Thur 5–10pm, Fri–Sat 9am–2pm and 5–11pm, Sun 9am–2pm and 5–9pm; $$$; bus: 22

Said by some to serve the best Italian food in the city: try the creamy polenta with wild-mushroom ragu, or the wild-boar tenderloin with gorgonzola sauce. A taste of Tuscany in the Pacific Northwest.

West Seattle

AMERICAN
Elliott Bay Brewery Pub
4720 California Avenue SW; tel: 206-932-8695; www.elliottbaybrewing.com; Mon–Sat 11am–midnight, Sun 11am–11pm; $; bus: 22, 85

West Seattle's brewpub serves good pub food (gourmet burgers, ahi tuna or Greek chicken gyro

sandwiches, as well as a selection of more than a dozen of their own beers, including No Doubt Stout, Elliott Bay IPA, and seasonal light ales.

Endolyne Joe's
9261 45th Avenue SW; tel: 206-937-joes; www.chowfoods.com; Mon–Fri 8.30am–10pm, Sat–Sun 8.30am–3pm and 5–10pm; $–$$; bus: 54

South of Colman Park, and up the hill from the Fauntleroy ferry terminal, this West Seattle restaurant changes its regional cuisine menu quarterly, from the French Quarter to tropical islands or Little Italy. American classics for breakfast, including fluffy pancakes, omelets and scrambles.

ITALIAN
La Rustica
4100 Beach Drive SW; tel: 206-932-3020; Tue–Sun 5–10pm; $$; bus: 37, 53

You have to hunt for La Rustica, located on beach drive well west of the main Alki drag, but the rustic Italian specialties are worth the search at this well-respected

ITALIAN
Madame K's
5327 Ballard Avenue NW; tel: 206-783-9710; Mon–Thur 5–10pm, Fri 5–11pm, Sat 4–11pm, Sun 4–9.30pm; $; bus: 44, 46

You might not imagine pizzas and bordellos going together, but in this vibrant red restaurant that once housed a brothel, Madame K has kept up appearances. Delicious,

Columbia City, La Medusa serves sensual Sicilian fare – often using fresh produce from the local farmers' market. They also own the Columbia City Bakery down the street.

Stellar Pizza (Georgetown)
5513 Airport Way; tel: 206-763-1660; www.stellarpizza.com; Mon 11am–11pm, Tue–Fri 11am–midnight, Sat 3pm–midnight, Sun 3–11pm; $; bus: 131, 134, 170

This family-owned pizza place in artsy Georgetown serves huge, hand-tossed pizzas, calzones, sandwiches, and pastas amid retro artifacts. Family-friendly, relaxed atmosphere, and the pizza smells out of this world. Good selection of beer and cocktails.

Tutta Bella (Columbia City)
4918 Rainier Avenue S; tel: 206-721-3501; www.tuttabella.com; Sun–Thur 11am–10pm, Sat–Sun 11am–11pm; $$; bus: 7, 9, 48

Authentic, wood-fired Neapolitan pizza is served at this eco-friendly and very popular pizzeria, where fresh, simple ingredients are combined to raise the art of pizza-making to a new high. Great atmosphere, including a bar where you can have a drink or an espresso and *gelato*.

neighborhood restaurant. Try the ricotta gnocchi with home-made sausage, wild boar, or lamb shank. Lovely, romantic, and cozy.

LATIN
Mission
2325 California Avenue SW; tel: 206-937-8220; daily 5pm–2am; $$; bus: 55, 85, 128

Some come to this kickin' West Seattle restaurant for the modern Latin cuisine (guacamole with plantains, fish and steak tacos, flan, Mexican ice cream) – others for the margaritas and the scene, both of which are best enjoyed late at night.

Other Great Neighborhoods

AMERICAN
Geraldine's Counter (Columbia City)
4872 Rainier Avenue S; tel: 206-723-2080; www.geraldinescounter.com; Tue–Thur 7am–9pm, Fri 7am–10pm, Sat 8am–10pm, Sun 8am–9pm; $; bus: 7, 9, 48

Breakfasts are a big hit here at this family-friendly hotspot in Columbia City

with big booths and big food. Lunch features staples such as mac and cheese and Kick Butt Chili, and for dinner try meatloaf or chicken pot pie. American comfort food done well.

5 Spot (Upper Queen Anne)
1502 Queen Anne Avenue N; tel: 206-285-spot; www.chowfoods.com; Mon–Fri 8.30am–midnight, Sat–Sun 8.30am–3pm and 5pm–midnight; $–$$; bus: 2, 13, 45

A terrific spot for breakfasts, on top of Queen Anne Hill. Be prepared to wait, though, because it's very popular and crowds form. The regularly changing menu features American fare from different regions in the country.

ITALIAN
La Medusa (Columbia City)
4857 Rainier Avenue S; tel: 206-723-2192; www.lamedusa restaurant.com; Tue and Thur 5–9pm, Wed, Fri and Sat 5–10pm; $$–$$$; bus: 7, 9, 48

One of the best-established restaurants in lively

Prices for a three-course dinner per person with half a bottle of wine:
$ = under $20
$$ = $20–45
$$$ = $45–60
$$$$ = more than $60

Shopping

Shoppers descend on Downtown every weekend to hit the department stores, shopping centers, and major chains, but there are also lots of great independent stores around town. Belltown has a wide array of boutiques and galleries, while Pioneer Square is full of galleries and antiques stores. Capitol Hill has trendy clothes and music stores, as does the U-District. Fremont and Ballard both have great shopping, from unique clothes to vintage furniture, while West Seattle combines boutiques with charming older stores. For specialist food stores, *see Food and Drink, p.56–7*; for active clothing, *see Outdoor Activities, p.91*.

Bookstores

Abraxis Books
5711 24th Avenue NW, Ballard; tel: 206-297-6777; www.abraxusbooks.com; Mon–Sat 10am–8pm, Sun until 6pm; bus: 18

Don't let the unprepossessing exterior of the old Ballard library put you off; this independent bookstore of new and mostly used books has a decent selection across all genres packed into the maze-like stacks. There are quiet nooks and crannies with overstuffed chairs in case you want to read before you buy.

Bailey-Coy Books
414 Broadway E, Capitol Hill; tel: 206-323-8842; www.bailey coybooks.com; Mon–Sat 10am–10pm, Sun 10am–8pm; bus: 9, 49, 60

Delightful Broadway bookstore with knowledgeable staff, great recommendations, and a good selection of gay literature as well as general literature. Also attractive gift cards.

Barnes and Noble
Pacific Place, 600 Pine Street, Downtown; tel: 206-264-0156; www.barnesandnoble.com; daily 9am–11pm; bus: 10, 12, 49; map p.133 D3

A huge selection of books, CDs, and magazines is available at this friendly and welcoming store Downtown. Its special events include author readings, signings, and there's also a coffee shop.

Borders Books & Music
1501 4th Avenue; tel: 206-622-4599; www.borders.com; Mon–Sat 8am–9pm, Sun 10am–8pm; bus: 1, 2, 13; map p.133 D3

Left: the famous Pike Place Market.

Seattle has a thriving literary scene, with frequent author events at local bookstores (especially Elliott Bay Book Company, *see left*, and the University Bookstore, *see below*), and the **Seattle Arts and Lectures** (www.lectures. org) series that draws big literary figures, such as Frank McCourt, Margaret Atwood, and John Updike, to Benaroya Hall.

Most major author tours include a stop in Seattle, where the written word is celebrated. Local talent is strong, too, with resident authors including **Robert Fulghum** (*All I Really Needed to Know I Learned in Kindergarten*, 1986), **David Guterson** (*Snow Falling on Cedars*, 1994), **Sherman Alexie** (*Indian Killer*, 1996), and **J.A. Jance** ('JP Beaumont' mysteries, 1985–). British-born **Jonathan Raban** (*Waxwings*, 2003) is among the literary crowd who settled here, and cartoonist **Gary Larson** of *The Far Side* also makes Seattle his home.

Seattle celebrity librarian Nancy Pearl is a regular literary commentator on National Public Radio's 'Morning Edition,' and on KUOW (94.9 FM).

Borders' Downtown store is well stocked across all genres and also has a music section.

Elliott Bay Book Company
101 S. Main Street, Pioneer Square; tel: 206-624-6600; www.elliottbaybook.com; Mon–Sat 9.30am–10pm, Sun 11am–7pm; bus: 15, 16, 18; map p.134 B3
Seattle's favorite independent bookstore, Elliott Bay is a warren of bookshelves, staff picks, and an amazing selection of new and used books.

Left: Bailey-Coy Books on Capitol Hill.

**Fremont Place
Book Company**
621 N. 35th Street, Fremont; tel: 206-547-5970; www.fremont placebooks.com; Mon–Sat 10am–8pm, Sun noon–6pm; bus: 26, 28, 31
A tiny, independent bookstore serving Fremont customers since 1989. They stock a little bit of everything, with an emphasis on fiction and politics.

**Ravenna Third
Place Books**
6504 20th Avenue NE, Ravenna; tel: 206-525-2347; www.ravenna thirdplace.com; Mon–Thur 8am–10pm, Fri–Sat 8am–11pm, Sun 8am–7pm; bus: 71, 72, 73
This is a magnet for booklovers, as well as beer- and coffee-drinkers, since the pub and bakery attract people who like to settle in for lively conversation. The store stocks a wide range of new and used books.

Secret Garden Books
2214 NW Market Street, Ballard; tel: 206-789-5006; www.secret gardenbooks.com; Mon–Fri 10am–8pm, Sat 10am–6pm, Sun noon–5pm; bus: 44, 46
This intimate full-service bookstore has an emphasis on children's books, and it caters to little visitors with small wooden tables and chairs. Another strength is the staff picks – recommendations in all their sections, from gardening to travel to fiction.

University Bookstore
4326 University Way NE, U-District; tel: 206-634-3400; www.bookstore.washington.edu; Mon–Fri 9am–9pm, Sat

10am–7pm, Sun noon–5pm; bus: 25, 44, 49

In addition to stocking required reading and supplies for students at the University of Washington, this large bookstore has a great selection of new and used books and also hosts author-readings and events.

Clothing

In addition to branches of many major retail chains that are located Downtown and in the malls, there are some interesting independent stores in every neighborhood, a selection of which are listed here.

Byrnie Utz Hats

310 Union Street, Downtown; tel: 206-623-0233; Mon–Sat 9.30am–5.30pm; bus: 1, 2, 16; map p.133 D2

In business since 1934, and maintaining an old-fashioned air of doing business, Byrnie Utz is the place to buy quality men's hats, from fedoras to Panama hats to Stetsons. Though not geared to women, there is a range of hats that fit across genders.

Canopy Blue

3121 E. Madison Street, Madison Valley; tel: 206-323-1115; www.canopyblue.com; Mon 11am–5pm, Tue–Fri 10am–7pm, Sat 10am–6pm, Sun noon–4pm; bus: 11, 84

Very expensive, very feminine, very cute clothes and accessories for women.

Crossroads Trading Company

325 Broadway E, Capitol Hill; tel: 206-328-5867; www.crossroads trading.com; daily 11am–7pm; bus: 9, 49, 60

Crossroads is one of the best thrift stores for affordable yet trendy second-hand clothes. Its buyers carefully sift through bags of clothing and select only recent fashions from big name labels such as Banana Republic, H&M, and J.Crew.

(Also at: 4300 University Way NE, U-District; tel: 206-632-3111.)

Encanto Barcelona

1406 1st Avenue, Downtown; tel: 206-621-1941; www.encantobarcelona.com; Mon–Sat 10am–7pm, Sun 11am–6pm; bus: 10, 12, 15; map p.136 A3

Stylish Spanish and urban European fashions for women and men.

Hip Zephyr

6421 Phinney Avenue N, Green Lake; tel: 206-905-6069; www.hipzephyr.com; Tue–Wed 11am–6pm and Fri, Thur 11am–8pm, Sun 11am–5pm; bus: 5

Hip Zephyr is a women's clothing boutique with an emphasis on European and American clothing, and classics with a twist. Jewelry, handbags, and accessories are also on offer.

Kuhlman

2419 1st Avenue, Belltown; tel: 206-441-1999; Mon–Sat 11am–7pm, Sun noon–6pm; bus: 15, 18, 21; map p.132 B4

Kuhlman stocks stylish menswear, from jeans to shirts, at this Belltown store and offers great service.

Les Amis

3420 Evanston Avenue N, Fremont; tel: 206-632-2877; www.lesamis-inc.com; Tue–Sat 11am–6pm, Sun 11am–5pm; bus: 28

This thoughtfully stocked boutique offers unique and beautiful designs by Diane Von Furstenburg, Trina Turk, and Theory, among others, as well as jewelry, lingerie, and gifts. Try to shop during one of its sales.

Right: A Mano sells excellent-quality leather shoes and bags.

Left: Downtown's
Encanto Barcelona.

Luly Yang
Studio Boutique
1218 4th Avenue, Downtown;
tel: 206-623-8200;
www.lulyyang.com; Mon–Sat
10am–6pm, Sun noon–5pm;
bus: 2, 13, 16; map p.133 D2
If money's no object,
exquisite bridal dresses,
dashing bespoke tuxedos,
elegant evening gowns, and
top-of-the-line accessories
can be yours at this Seattle
designer's sumptuous
Downtown boutique. If your
budget doesn't stretch this
far, just gaze admiringly at
the gorgeous window
displays.

Metro
231 Broadway E, Capitol Hill;
tel: 206-726-7978; Mon–Sat
11am–10pm, Sun noon–5pm;
bus: 9, 49, 60
The leather, vinyl, fishnets,
and general fetishwear pull in
drag queens and Goths alike.
A good selection of patent
leather platforms and accessories, too.

Nordstrom Rack
1601 2nd Avenue, Downtown;
tel: 206-448-8522;
www.nordstrom.com; Mon–Sat
9.30am–9pm, Sun 10am–7pm;
bus: 10, 12, 15; map p.136 A2
Always crowded, always long
lines, but the bargains on
cut-price Nordstrom apparel,
shoes, and housewares
makes it worth enduring the
crush.

Red Light
312 Broadway Avenue E, Capitol
Hill; tel: 206-329-2200; www.
redlightvintage.com; Mon–Thur
11am–8pm, Fri–Sat 11am–9pm,
Sun 11am–7pm; bus: 9, 49, 60
Great consignment and vintage clothing store on Broadway for men and women. You
can find it by the entertain-
ingly dressed and staged
mannequins in the window.
They stock a wide assort-
ment of interesting clothes,
and appeal to students,
party-goers, and anyone who
wants to be a little different.

Sweetie
4508 California Avenue SW,
West Seattle; tel: 206-923-3533;
www.sweetieboutique.com;

Outdoor gear and Seattle go
hand-in-hand, with big names
like **Eddie Bauer** and **REI**
originating here. *See Outdoor
Activities, p.91.*

Mon–Fri 11am–7pm, Sat
11am–6pm, Sun 11am–5pm;
bus: 55, 85
A hip little boutique with
trendy casual wear to sophisticated evening wear for
women.

Value Village
1525 11th Avenue, Capitol Hill;
tel: 206-322-7789; www.value
village.com; Mon–Sat 9am–9pm,
Sun 11am–7pm; bus: 10, 11, 49
A well-stocked, enormous
second-hand store selling all
sorts of clothes, shoes, and
household goods.

SHOES
A Mano
1115 1st Avenue, Downtown;
tel: 206-292-1767; www.shopa
mano.com; Mon–Sat
10am–6pm, Sun noon–5pm;
bus: 10, 12, 15; map p.133 D1
A Mano offers a small but
select range of gorgeous

Left: Downtown has a branch of the famous New York department store.

women's shoes, handbags, and jewelry, all at high-end prices.

Clementine
4447 California Avenue SW, West Seattle; tel: 206-935-9400; Mon–Fri 11am–7pm, Sat 10am–6pm, Sun 11am–5pm; bus: 55, 85

Fabulous women's shoes, largely from Europe and Brazil, as well as handbags and jewelry by Northwest designers line the shelves of this small West Seattle shoe boutique.

John Fluevog Shoes
205 Pine Street, Downtown; tel: 206-441-1065; www.fluevog.com; Mon–Sat 11am–7pm, Sun 11am–6pm; bus: 10, 12, 49; map p.136 A2

You'll find handmade contemporary styles for both men and women at this funky shoe store.

Re-Soul
5319 Ballard Avenue, Ballard; tel: 206-789-7312; www.resoul.com; Mon–Sat 11am–6pm, Sun noon–5pm; bus: 44, 46

Cool shoes for men and women, carefully chosen for each season, as well as some interesting and well-designed miscellaneous stuff such as vintage telephones, birdhouses, and modern furniture.

Shoefly
2030 1st Avenue, Belltown; tel: 206-729-763; www.shoefly.com; Mon–Fri 11am–7pm, Sat–Sun 11am–6pm; bus: 15, 18, 21; map p.136 A1

Shoefly is a stylish boutique for women's and men's shoes as well as handbags and jewelry.

Department Stores and Shopping Malls

Downtown Seattle is well served by upscale shopping centers and two department stores: Nordstrom and Macy's. All offer cafés and dining options, and area parking garages are easy to come by. University Village offers a more relaxed shopping experience in the U-District.

Macy's
3rd Avenue and Pine Street, Downtown; tel: 206-506-6000; www.macys.com; Mon–Wed 10am–8pm, Thur–Sat

10am–9pm, Sun 11am–7pm; bus: 10, 12, 49; map p.133 C3

The New York department store has perfumes and cosmetics, handbags, and shoes on the ground floor, menswear downstairs, and two floors of women's fashion. There's also a good range of home furnishings, from crystal and china to sofas and mattresses.

Nordstrom
500 Pine Street, Downtown; tel: 206-628-2111; www.nordstrom.com; Mon–Sat 9.30am–9pm, Sun 11am–7pm; bus: 10, 12, 49; map p.133 D3

Seattle's premier department store, and the only home-grown one to survive, Nordstrom started out as a high-quality shoe store, and shoes continue to be one of the big attractions here, with big designer names and big price tags to match. Also of note are the ladies' fashion and lingerie departments, and quality clothing for men. Excellent customer service.

Pacific Place
600 Pine Street, Downtown; tel: 206-405-2655; www.pacificplaceseattle.com; Mon–Sat 9.30am–9pm, Sun 11am–7pm;

Right: shoppers in Seattle-born Nordstrom; outside dining at Westlake Center.

Shopping is fun and easy for visitors to the Emerald City, since the Downtown retail center is close to most major hotels. And why not treat yourself to some pampering afterwards at one of the many spas? *See Pampering, p.92–3.*

bus: 10, 12, 49; map p.133 D3

This glitzy shopper's paradise with glass ceiling and marble floors is home to premium stores, including Tiffany's, Cartier, Barney's New York, Restoration Hardware, Ann Taylor, and Coach, among many others. On the top floor are restaurants, bars, and movie theaters.

Rainier Square
1333 5th Avenue, Downtown; www.rainier-square.com; daily, hours vary by store; bus: 12, 13, 70; map p.133 D2

This small shopping center in the base of the Rainier Tower *(see p.27)* offers boutique shopping at Brooks Brothers, Escada, Louis Vuitton, and other high-end stores. Also here is the Seattle Architecture Foundation, if you're interested in learning more about the buildings in Seattle.

University Village
NE 45th Street and 25th Avenue NE, U-District; tel: 206-523-0622; www.uvillage.com; Mon–Sat 9.30am–9pm, Sun 11am–6pm; bus: 25, 65, 68

U-Village is an open-air lifestyle shopping center, where you walk between the buildings (helping yourself to a complimentary umbrella when needed). Crate and Barrel, Eddie Bauer, Gap, Aveda, Victoria's Secrets, Barnes and Noble, and many more stores and places to eat.

Westlake Center
400 Pine Street, Downtown; tel: 206-467-1600; www.west

lakecenter.com; Mon–Sat 10am–9pm, Sun 11am–6pm; bus: 10, 12, 49; map p.133 D3

With four levels of shopping, a reasonably priced food court with lots of choices, and being right Downtown (with the monorail station on the top floor), Westlake Center is always busy. Made in Washington has quality souvenirs, and other stores include Nine West, Claire's Accessories, Talbot's, Fossil, and Lush.

Furniture and Furnishings

Area 51
401 E. Pine Street, Capitol Hill; tel: 206-568-4782; www.area51seattle.com; Mon–Fri noon–6.30pm, Sat 11am–6pm, Sun noon–5pm; bus: 14, 43, 49

Area 51 has a great selection of both modern and vintage retro furniture at good prices. Its airy showroom features lamps, vases, glassware, and knick-knacks. They also buy vintage pieces from the public.

Capers
4521 California Avenue SW, West Seattle; tel: 206-932-0371; Mon–Fri 7am–8pm, Sat 7am–6pm, Sun 7am–5pm; bus: 55, 85

Friendly assistants greet you at this store that stocks good-quality sofas, chairs, tables, and beds, as well as beautiful soft furnishings and linens. There are glasses,

coasters, and other housewares that make good gifts.

Retrofit Home
1419 12th Avenue, Capitol Hill; tel: 206-568-4663; www.retrofithome.com; Mon–Fri 11am–6pm, Sat noon–7pm, Sun noon–4pm; bus: 11, 12

From armless couches to leather chaises longues, polka-dot pillows to retro lamps, this hip furniture and accessories shop melds the clean, mod lines of the '60s and sleek contemporary designs.

Gifts

Archie McPhee
2428 NW Market Street, Ballard; tel: 206-297-0240; www.mcphee.com; Mon–Sat 10am–7pm, Sun 11am–6pm; bus: 44, 46

Great for a whole range of tacky and kitsch toys, practical jokers and teenage boys will love this store, but there's usually something for the rest of us here, too, from boxing nuns to jumbo handlebar moustaches to wind-up hopping lederhosen.

Bitters & Co.
513 N. 36th Street, Fremont; tel: 206-632-0886; www.bittersco.com; Tue–Sat 11am–6pm, Sun noon–5pm; bus: 26, 28, 31

In an old Fremont building with whitewashed wooden

Right: glitzy Pacific Place.

walls and ceiling, two sisters showcase the textiles, pottery, cards, jewelry, dinnerware, and furniture that they source from the Philippines, Guatemala, Portugal, Mexico, Morocco, and the US. With a focus on environmentally sustainable products, they support small artisans who don't have another outlet.

Frank and Dunya
3418 Fremont Ave N, Fremont; tel: 206-547-6760; daily 11am–7pm; bus: 26, 28, 31
This Fremont gift store sells the work of local artists, whether paintings, cards, jewelry, or pottery. Almost all of the products are made by Washington artists.

Harem
618 Broadway E, Capitol Hill; tel: 206-329 0228; www.seattle harem.com; Wed–Mon noon–10pm; bus: 9, 49, 60
Middle Eastern-inspired gifts, clothing, and furnishings are sold at this lovely store on the north end of Broadway. You can find accessories for belly dancing, jewelry, and home accents such as candles and throw cushions.

Moxie Paper Goods and Gifts
3916 California Avenue SW, West Seattle; tel: 206-932-2800; www.moxiepapergoods.com; Tue–Fri 10am–7pm, Sat–Sun 10am–5pm; bus: 55, 85
Modern and attractive cards, chic wrapping supplies, and contemporary stationery are available at this great West Seattle shop.

Markets

At the famous **Pike Place Market** you can buy fresh produce, fish, meats, cheeses, flowers, and a wide array of gifts. But many neighborhoods also have farmers' markets (www.seattle farmersmarkets.org), where you can stock up on the best local and organic ingredients, and get the flavor of a neighborhood. The Fremont Market is more of a flea market with arts and crafts, clothing, vintage furniture, and some food.

Ballard Farmers' Market
Ballard Avenue NW, Ballard; Nov–Apr: Sun 11am–3pm, May–Oct: Sun 10am–4pm; bus: 44, 46

Broadway Farmers' Market
Broadway and E. Thomas Street, Capitol Hill; mid-May–mid-Nov: Sun 11am–3pm; bus: 9, 49, 60

> **Pike Place Market** is a great starting point for ethnic gifts, Northwest original arts and crafts, and a whole host of amazing fresh food. To avoid the swarming masses, it's best to visit on a weekday morning. Come for a late breakfast or nibble your way from one stall to another.

Right: cut flowers and vegetables at Pike Place Market.

Left: Fremont's Deluxe Junk is great for a rummage.

Columbia City Farmers' Market
Rainier Avenue S and S. Edmunds Street, Columbia City; May–late Oct: Wed 3–7pm; bus: 7, 9, 48

Fremont Sunday Market
400 N 34th Street, Fremont; tel: 206-781-6776; www.fremontmarket.com; Apr–Oct: Sun 10am–5pm, Nov–Mar: Sun 10am–4pm; bus: 28

Pike Place Market
Pike Place and 1st Avenue, Downtown; www.pikeplace market.org; Mon–Sat 10am–6pm, Sun 11am–5pm; bus: 10, 12, 15; map p.136 A1–B3

Pike Place Market is perennially popular with tourists, who are captivated by the fishmongers and their flying fish at **Pike Place Fish**, the reasonably priced bouquets from the Hmong farmers, a great selection of bulk teas and spices at Market Spice, and a host of mouthwatering comestibles. There are also buskers aplenty, friendly vendors, as well as shops selling unique art, clothing, and jewelry.

The market has different levels, with permanent and specialty stores downstairs and across the street (including the original **Starbucks** at 1912 Pike Place) where you can buy exotic imported textiles, Indian spices, precision knives, music memorabilia, and many other goodies.

U-District Farmers' Market
University Way and NE 50th, U-District; year-round: Sat 9am–2pm; bus: 70, 71, 72

West Seattle Farmers' Market
California Avenue SW and SW Alaska Street, West Seattle; year-round: Sun 10am–2pm; bus: 55, 85

Vintage and Antiques

Deluxe Junk
3518 Fremont Place, Fremont; tel: 206-634-2733; Fri–Sun 11.30am–5.30pm; bus: 26, 28, 31

A step up from most vintage stores, Deluxe Junk sources retro furniture, vintage ball gowns and tuxedos, old cameras, the occasional motorcycle, and many other gems.

> Go green and bring a shopping bag to the markets with you; our trees and landfill sights will thank you.

Fremont Vintage Mall
3419 Fremont Place N, Fremont; tel: 206-548-9140; www.freemontvintagemall.com; Mon–Sat 11am–7pm, Sun 11am–6pm; bus: 26, 28, 31

It's easy to miss this underground treasure trove, since there's only an unassuming door at street level. But a wander downstairs may just lead to that certain something – a teak table or that '70s record you remember from your childhood – you can't live without.

Pioneer Square Antique Mall
602 1st Avenue, Pioneer Square; tel: 206-624-1164; www. pioneersquareantiques.com; Mon–Sat 10.30am–5.30pm, Sun noon–5pm; bus: 15, 18; map p.134 B4

Over 60 dealers sell a wide range of vintage and antique silver, pottery, jewelry, toys, and books at this warren of an underground mall in the center of historic Pioneer Square.

Spectator Sports

Seattleites love their sports, and you're sure to know whenever a major home game is happening because traffic crawls to a standstill. The city is currently home to five professional sports teams – the Seahawks (football), Mariners (baseball), Storm (women's basketball), Thunderbirds (hockey), and Sounders (soccer). Sadly, in 2008 the city lost the beloved Seattle Sonics after new owners moved to the men's basketball team to Oklahoma City, much to the chagrin of local fans. The area is also home to horse racing, auto racing, and lots of regattas on the beautiful waterways. *See also Outdoor Activities, p.86–91.*

Auto Racing

Evergreen Speedway
14405 179th Avenue SE, Monroe; tel: 360-805-6100; evergreenspeedway.com
Located on the Evergreen Fairgrounds in Monroe, 33 miles (53km) northeast of Seattle, the NASCAR Elite Division Northwest Series events are held here, as are local and national races from March through October.

Baseball

Seattle Mariners
Safeco Field, 1st Avenue S; tel: 206-346-4000; www. mariners.com; bus: 28, 39, 56; map p.134 B1

In late April or early May the opening day of boating season is celebrated with the **Windermere Cup Rowing Regatta**, in conjunction with the Seattle Yacht Club and the University of Washington. Thousands of spectators line the Montlake Cut in the U-District to watch collegiate crew racing with national and international crew teams, followed by a colorful boat parade.

Safeco Field, the $417-million ballpark, mixes tradition with high tech, with real grass on the playing field and a spectacular retractable roof, an engineering marvel unto itself. Come and watch the Mariners at one of their many home games from April through September.

Basketball

Seattle Storm
KeyArena, Seattle Center; tel: 206-281-5800; www. wnba.com/storm; bus: 1, 2, 15; map p.130 A2
Seattle's WNBA (Women's National Basketball League) team plays at KeyArena during the NBA off-season. In 2008 the team was sold to Force 10 Hoops, comprised of local businesswomen Anne Levinson, Ginny Gilder, Lisa Brummel, and Dawn Trudeau, thus securing the Storm's home in Seattle.

Until July 2008 the Men's NBA team – the Seattle Sonics – played the Key Arena, with the strong support of fans. But after the team was sold by Starbucks CEO Howard Schultz to an Oklahoma group, headed by Clay Bennett, the new owners successfully petitioned to move the team to Oklahoma City. Despite strong and impassioned legal challenges, the move was upheld, and the Sonics left town. The team's name and colors, however, remain in Seattle, with hopes that a new NBA team will be found.

Huskies Basketball
Bank of America Arena at Hec Edmundson Pavilion, University of Washington; tel: 206-543-2200; www.gohuskies.com; bus: 243
The UW basketball season begins in November and ends in March for both men's and women's. The Bank of America Arena is a decent facility, and the men's team in particular is rising in national prominence.

Football

Seattle Seahawks
Qwest Field; tel: 1-888-nfl-

Right: Qwest Field, home of the Seahawks and Sounders.

Left: the Mariners in action at the Safeco Field.

Hockey

Seattle Thunderbirds
KeyArena, Seattle Center; tel: 206-448-puck; www.seattle-thunderbirds.com; bus: 1, 2, 15; map p.130 A2
Season runs from late September to March (or May if they make the play-offs).

Horse Racing

Emerald Downs
2300 Emerald Downs Drive, Auburn; tel: 253-288-7000; www.emdowns.com
Located in Auburn (25 miles/40km south of Seattle) on 167 acres (67 hectares), this thoroughbred racetrack has events from April through September, including special hat and mascot days, and fireworks on the 4th of July.

Soccer

Seattle Sounders
Qwest Field; tel: 1-800-796-kick; www.seattlesounders.net; bus: 15, 18, 28; map p.134 B2
The 2005 USL First Division champions play their season from April to October. They share Qwest Field with the Seahawks football team.

Every Tuesday evening during summer Lake Union is home to the **Duck Dodge**, a high-spirited sailing regatta that whizzes around and around the lake. The best vantage point is GasWorks Park *(see p.95)*: bring a picnic and settle in to watch. Great views of Downtown, too!

---

hawk/635-4295; www.seahawks.com; bus: 15, 18, 28; map p.134 B2

Seattle's NFL (National Football League) team plays at state-of-the-art Qwest Field.
Huskies Football
Husky Stadium, University of Washington; tel: 206-543-2200; gohuskies.cstv.com; bus: 243
Home to the University of Washington Huskies Football team, the 72,500-seat Husky Stadium has the added attraction of offering views of Lake Washington and the Cascade Mountains.

Theater and Dance

Theater has well-established roots in Seattle, with a savvy audience dedicated to everything from fringe to top-notch traveling shows. The city has a reputation as the Broadway capital of the West Coast, with many Broadway-bound shows premiering in Seattle. Dance, too, is highly regarded. In the 1970s, a generation of aspiring choreographers moved to Seattle to perform and study with acclaimed modern-dance choreographer Bill Evans. Since then, dance has found a sturdy foundation on Seattle stages.

Theater

Seattle has its fair share of established theaters showing the usual rota of Broadway-style hits. However, professional performances can also be found in the more intimate settings of smaller theaters. **Intiman Theatre** and **Seattle Shakespeare Company**, at the Seattle Center, specialize respectively in revivals and productions of the Bard. But don't expect lowbrow performances at these smaller venues. Intiman premiered *A Light in the Piazza*, which later garnered numerous

Several venues offer a 'Pay What You Will' night, where you decide what you'll pay (anything above a dollar) for a show. These nights are usually advertised on their website up to two weeks before the event.

Tony Awards in New York and toured the country.

While many fringe and alternative theaters have come and gone, others have found a loyal audience in Seattle's discerning and culturally inclined crowd. A selection of the best venues is listed below.

Right: *Fathers and Sons* performed at ACT.

5th Avenue Theatre
1308 5th Avenue, Downtown; tel: 206-625-1900; www.5th avenuetheatre.org; bus: 11, 14, 70; map p.133 D2
This spectacularly ornate Chinese-themed theater built in 1926 and beautifully renovated in 1980 stages show-stopping Broadway-style shows and musical theater. It was here that *Hairspray*, which went on to win eight Tony Awards, and *The Wedding Singer* premiered for Seattleites before finding glory in New York.

A Contemporary Theatre (ACT)
Kreielsheimer Place, 700 Union Street, Downtown; tel: 206-292-7676; www.acttheatre.org; bus: 10, 11, 49; map p.133 E3
Since the mid-1960s this non-profit theater company has been commissioning new works and staging outstanding contemporary the-

Left: a performance at the Intiman Theatre. **Right:** the Annex Theatre in Capitol Hill.

Left: *Seven Brides for Seven Brothers* at 5th Avenue Theatre.

Full-price tickets to most shows in town are available through the box office of the theater or through Ticketmaster (tel: 206-628-0888; www.ticketmaster.com). Ticket-window sells online tickets (www.ticketwindowonline.com) or half-price day-of-show tickets (cash only) at Ticket Ticket, located in the Pike Place Market information booth at 1st Avenue and Pine Street.

ater that strives to address social issues and cultural boundaries. From annual favorites like *A Christmas Carol* (first staged at ACT in 1976), to world premieres that have gone on to New York (like *Scent of the Roses* and *In the Penal Colony*), it's no wonder ACT's 10,000 subscribers continue coming back for more.

Annex Theatre
1100 E. Pike Street, Capitol Hill; tel: 206-728-0933; www.annex theatre.org; bus: 11, 12, 49
This well-established fringe theater, around since the 1980s, is dedicated to staging bold and experimental works with around 10 shows a year.

Intiman Theatre Company
201 S. Mercer Street, Seattle Center; tel: 206-269-1900; www.intiman.org; bus: 3, 4; map p.130 A3
Founded in 1972 by Margaret Booker, who studied in Sweden with Ingmar Bergman and Alf Sjöberg, Intiman is named after the Swedish word for 'intimate,' a description that fits this small, well-respected Seattle Center theater. Under the guidance of Tony Award-winning artistic director, Bartlett Sher, new life is being breathed into the classics such as *To Kill a Mockingbird* and *A Streetcar Named Desire*.

Market Theater
1428 Post Alley, Pike Place Market; tel: 206-781-9273; www.unexpectedproductions. org; bus: 10, 12, 15; map p.136 A3
Unexpected Productions theater troupe makes its home here with the town's best improv, including satire, spoofs, and serious drama.

Moore Theatre
1932 2nd Avenue, Belltown; tel: 206-443-1744; www.the moore.com; bus: 15, 18, 21; map p.133 C3
This historic theater (1907) hosts a rotating line-up of everything from off-Broadway shows to live music, and stand-up comics, and is the performance space for Spectrum Dance Theater.

Paramount Theatre

911 Pine Street, Downtown; tel: 206-467-5510; www.the paramount.com; bus: 10, 12, 49; map p.133 E3

The unmissable retro neon sign and marquee outside illuminate this beautifully restored grand old theater, which draws large crowds for award-winning shows and traveling companies and performers, as well as top names in music and comedy. Expect to find international hits like *Mamma Mia*.

Seattle Repertory Theatre

155 Mercer Street, Seattle Center; tel: 206-443-2222; www.seattlerep.org; bus: 3, 4; map p.130 A3

One of America's premier non-profit resident theatres, Seattle Repertory Theatre is an internationally recognized, Tony Award-winning regional theater with an audience of 130,000 each season.

The Seattle Rep performs at two venues: the larger Bagley Wright Theatre and more intimate Leo K Theatre.

Seattle Shakespeare Company

Center House Theatre, 1st Floor Center House, Seattle Center;

tel: 206-733-8222; www.seattle shakespeare.org; bus: 3, 4; map p.130 B2

Committed to staging three Shakespearean plays, as well as one classic and one new play each season, Seattle Shakespeare Company performs at a variety of venues, including the Center House Theatre in the Seattle Center.

Theater Schmeater

1500 Summit Avenue, Capitol Hill; tel: 206-324-5801; www.schmeater.org; bus: 10, 12, 14

Housed in a former parking garage, this space offers a fun mix of serious theater and goof-ball late-night shows like the popular *Twilight Zone – Live on Stage*.

Dance

Century Ballroom

915 E. Pine Street, 2nd floor, Capitol Hill; tel: 206-324-7263; www.centuryballroom.com; bus: 9, 49, 60

Check out phenomenal salsa, lindy hop, and swing dancers at this gracious old ballroom, which puts on occasional talent from New York, LA, and other dance capitals in between the regular public dances and classes it offers.

On the Boards

100 W. Roy Street, Queen Anne; tel: 206-217-9888; www.onthe boards.org; bus: 1, 2, 8

Left: African dance troupe Compagnie Heddy Maalem performing at the Paramount Theatre.

Recognized as one of the first institutions in the country to premiere experimental modern works by both national and international artists, On the Boards – nearly three decades old – is Seattle's premier contemporary performance organization. Experimental, often mixed-media shows that combine dance, theater, and art, are presented in one of two performance spaces at this arts center on Lower Queen Anne.

It showcases breakthrough performances by local artists in its spring **Northwest New Works Festival** and **12 Minutes Max**, which highlights emerging artists, around six times a year.

Pacific Northwest Ballet
301 Mercer Street, Queen Anne; tel: 206-441-2424; www.pnb.org; bus: 3, 4
When Marion Oliver McCaw Hall is not in use for operas, you can enjoy performances by Seattle's celebrated ballet

Reviews and up-to-date information on shows can be found in the *Seattle PI* and *The Seattle Times*, as well as the free weeklies *The Stranger* and *Seattle Weekly*, published on Thursdays. Newspapers are available on the street, in coffee shops, bars, bookstores, and grocery stores.

company, which draws the highest per-capita dance attendance in the country. There are at least six productions from October to May. Led by artistic director Peter Boal, the ballet's active repertoire includes classics such as *Swan Lake* and the popular annual performance of *Nutcracker*, choreographed by founding artistic director Kent Stowell, with sets designed by children's-book illustrator Maurice Sendak *(Where the Wild Things Are)*.

Spectrum Dance Theater
800 Lake Washington Blvd, Madrona; tel: 206-325-4161; www.spectrumdance.org; bus: 2, 27
The state's largest professional contemporary dance

company, Spectrum Dance Theater, has garnered national and international attention. When the company is not touring, it holds most of its performances at the Moore Theatre *(see p.123)*.

Velocity Dance Center
915 E. Pine Street, Suite 200, Capitol Hill; tel: 206-325-8773; www.velocitydancecenter.org; bus: 49
This non-profit contemporary dance organization offers classes and attracts great talent. Performances are often held at the nearby **Broadway Performance Hall** (1625 Broadway E, Capitol Hill).

Burlesque

A major revival in burlesque has hit the Seattle stage, with almost nightly performances somewhere in town. This funny, light-hearted art of the tease stops just shy of nudity and is a body-positive celebration of the (mostly) female form. Among the successful artists are the **Atomic Bombshells**, the **Von Foxies**, **Miss Indigo Blue**, and **Waxy Moon**. Some of the more popular venues include:

Columbia City Theater
4916 Rainier Avenue, Columbia City; tel: 206-723-0088; www.columbiacitytheater.com; bus: 7, 9, 48

The Pink Door
1919 Post Alley, Pike Place Market; tel: 206-443-3241; www.thepinkdoor.net; bus: 10, 12, 15; map p.136 A2

Re-Bar
1114 Howell Street, Downtown; tel: 206-233-9873; www.rebarseattle.com; bus: 25, 66; map p.133 E4

Left: the Theater Schmeater bar and its performance of *The Wind in the Willows.*

Transportation

Getting to Seattle is easy, with all major US airlines and many international carriers serving Seattle-Tacoma International Airport. Amtrak offers good rail links, and Greyhound has extensive bus connections with other US cities. Once you've arrived, a good system of buses, streetcars, and even a monorail will get you around Seattle. There are also decent bike lanes, and many neighborhoods are well suited to walking. For excursions beyond the city, a car offers the most flexibility and convenience, but there are also ferries or floatplanes to transport you to the islands.

Getting There

BY AIR

Sea-Tac Airport is 13 miles (20km) south of Seattle. **Grayline** (tel: 206-624-5077) and **Quick Shuttle** (tel: 1-800-665-2122) provide shuttle service to major Downtown hotels; **Shuttle Express** (tel: 206-622-1424) offers door-to-door service throughout the Greater Seattle area. A taxi ride to Downtown costs around $30. **Metro Transit**'s bus 194 provides express service for $2.25 (peak times). In late 2009, **Sound Transit** (tel: 206-398-5000) is due to begin service on its light rail link to Downtown.

BY BUS

Greyhound
811 Stewart Street, Downtown; tel: 1-800-231-2222; www.greyhound.com
Comprehensive service of scheduled routes across the US.

Green Tortoise
Tel: 1-800-867-8647; www.greentortoise.com
Fun, alternative service between San Francisco, Portland, and Seattle.

Quick Shuttle
Tel: 1-800-665-2122; www.quickcoach.com
Express service between Vancouver, BC and Seattle.

BY TRAIN

King Street Station at 303 S. Jackson Street, Pioneer Square, is the depot for Amtrak trains (tel: 1-800-usarail; www.amtrak.com), which connect Seattle with Portland, San Francisco, and LA on the scenic Coast Starlight; with Vancouver, BC on the Cascades; and with Chicago on the Empire Builder.

BY CAR

Major freeways into Seattle are Interstate 5 (I 5), which stretches from the Canadian to the Mexican borders, and I 90, which connects to the East Coast.

Getting Around

PUBLIC TRANSPORTATION
Metro Transit operates an extensive bus service. Exact fare is required: $1.75 during peak trips (6–9am, 3–6pm weekdays) and $1.50 off-peak. Ask for a transfer so you can catch a connecting bus for free. Downtown is a 'Ride

Left: the Monorail is a great way to see the city center, or you can take the green route and cycle.

Left: commuters in Downtown's transit tunnel.

credit card, valid driver's license, and to be 25 years of age.

Some rules to remember while driving: it's illegal to use a hand-held cell phone; right turns are permitted on red lights after coming to a complete stop; when parking on steep hills curb your wheels and set the emergency brake to prevent runaway vehicles; obey the parking signs or you'll risk getting a ticket.

FERRIES

An extensive system of ferries connects points across Puget Sound, including popular runs from Seattle to Bainbridge or Vashon Islands. The privately run **Victoria Clipper** provides passenger-only service to Victoria, BC.

Victoria Clipper
Tel: 1-800-888-2535;
www.clippervacations.com
Washington State Ferries
Tel: 206-464-6400;
www.wsdot.wa/gov/ferries

AIR
Kenmore Air
tel: 866-435-9524;
www.kenmoreair.com
Kenmore Air flies floatplanes between Seattle's Lake Union and the San Juan Islands, as well as Victoria, BC.

What better way to offset the costs of your carbon footprint racked in getting to Seattle than to use foot- or pedal-power to get around the city? Seattle has some scenic bike routes (you can even hook your bike onto the front of Metro buses to travel farther), and most neighborhoods are friendly for walkers. Downtown's 'Ride Free Zone' makes it easy to hop on and off public transit whenever your feet need a break. *See also Outdoor Activities, p.86–7, 89–90.*

Free Zone' where bus journeys are free. For schedules and services, contact Metro (tel: 206-553-3000; http://transit.metrokc.gov).

The **South Lake Union Streetcar** provides service between Downtown and South Lake Union, and the **Monorail** runs between Downtown's Westlake Center and the Seattle Center.

TAXIS

There are taxi stands at major hotels, bus depots, train stations, and the airport. You can also flag one down in the street, or call to request a pick-up.
Farwest Cab
Tel: 206-622-1717
Orange Cab
Tel: 206-522-8800
Yellow Cab
Tel: 206-622-6500

CAR RENTAL AND DRIVING
Avis (tel: 1-800-831-2847), **Enterprise** (tel: 1-800-736 8222), and **Hertz** (tel: 1-800-654-3131) are among the national car rental agencies with offices at Sea-Tac and Downtown. To rent a car you'll need a major

Right: Downtown buses.

Atlas

The following streetplan of Seattle makes it easy to find the attractions listed in our A–Z section. A selective index to streets and sights will help you find other locations throughout the city.

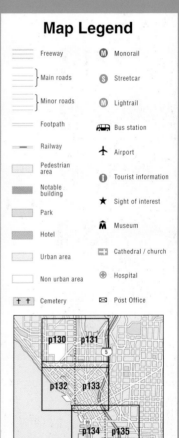

Map Legend

Freeway		Ⓜ	Monorail
Main roads		Ⓢ	Streetcar
Minor roads		Ⓜ	Lightrail
Footpath		🚌	Bus station
Railway		✈	Airport
Pedestrian area		ⓘ	Tourist information
Notable building		★	Sight of interest
Park		𝗠̂	Museum
Hotel		⊞	Cathedral / church
Urban area		⊕	Hospital
Non urban area		✉	Post Office
Cemetery			

p130 p131

p132 p133

p134 p135

Pike Place Market   p136

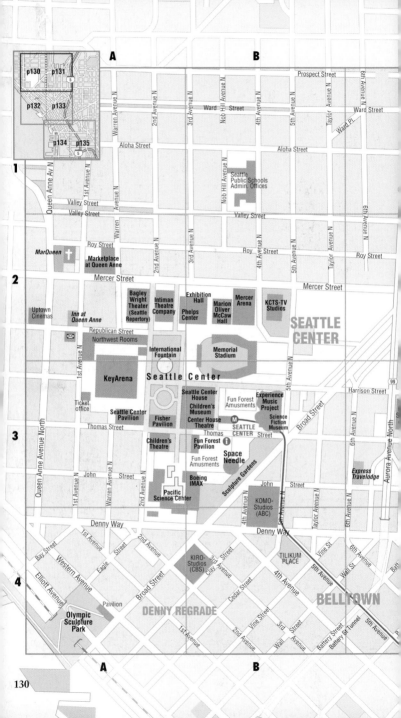

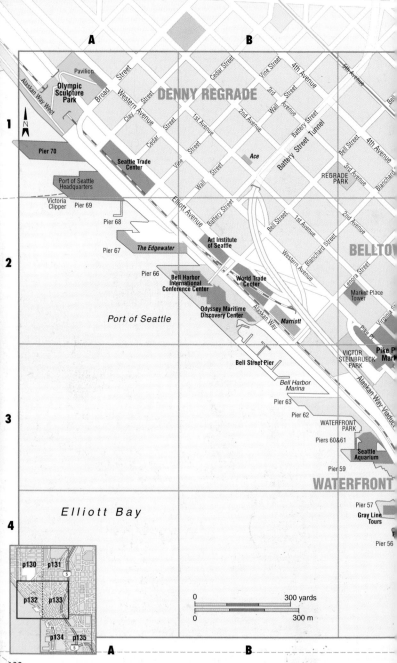

Cedar Street

Broad Street

Western Avenue

Pavilion

Olympic Sculpture Park

Alaskan Way West

DENNY REGRADE

Vine Street

4th Avenue

3rd Street

5th Avenue

Clay Street

Cedar Street

1st Avenue

2nd Avenue

Wall Avenue

Battery Street

1

Pier 70

Seattle Trade Center

Vine Street

Wall Street

Ace

Battery Street Tunnel

Bell Street

4th Avenue

3rd Avenue

Blanchard

REGRADE PARK

Port of Seattle Headquarters

Victoria Clipper

Pier 69

Elliott Avenue

Battery Street

Bell Street

1st Avenue

2nd Avenue

Pier 68

2

Pier 67

The Edgewater

Art Institute of Seattle

Western Avenue

Blanchard Street

BELLTOW

Lenora Street

Pier 66

Bell Harbor International Conference Center

World Trade Center

Market Place Tower

Virginia S

Port of Seattle

Odyssey Maritime Discovery Center

Alaskan Way

Marriott

Pike Pa

VICTOR STEINBRUECK PARK

Pike P Mar

Bell Street Pier

Alaskan Way Viaduct

Bell Harbor Marina

3

Pier 63

Pier 62

WATERFRONT PARK

Piers 60 & 61

Seattle Aquarium

Pier 59

WATERFRONT

Elliott Bay

Pier 57

Gray Line Tours

4

Pier 56

p130	p131
p132	p133
p134	p135

0   300 yards

0   300 m

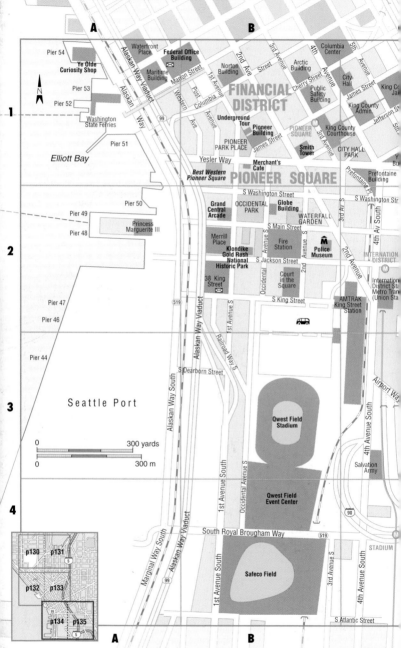

Pier 54

Ye Olde
Curiosity Shop

Pier 53

Pier 52

Waterfront
Place

Federal Office
Building

Maritime
Building

Norton
Building

Arctic
Building

Columbia
Center

City
Hall

King Cc
Jai

King County
Admin.

Washington
State Ferries

**FINANCIAL
DISTRICT**

Cherry Street

Public
Safety
Building

James Street

King County
Courthouse

Jefferson S

Pier 51

Underground
Tour

Pioneer
Building

PIONEER
SQUARE

Smith
Tower

CITY HALL
PARK

Elliott Bay

PIONEER
PARK PLACE

James Street

Yesler Way

Best Western
Pioneer Square

Merchant's
Cafe

Prefontaine
Building

PIONEER SQUARE

S Washington Street

S Washington Str

Pier 50

Pier 49

Grand
Central
Arcade

OCCIDENTAL
PARK

Globe
Building

WATERFALL
GARDEN

Pier 48

Princess
Marguerite III

S Main Street

Merrill
Place

Klondike
Gold Rush
National
Historic Park

Fire
Station

Police
Museum

INTERNATION
DISTRICT

S Jackson Street

Pier 47

38 King
Street

Court
in the
Square

S King Street

Internation
District Sta
Metro Tran
(Union Sta

Pier 46

AMTRAK
King Street
Station

Pier 44

Seattle Port

S Dearborn Street

| 0 | | 300 yards |
| 0 | | 300 m |

Qwest Field
Stadium

Salvation
Army

Qwest Field
Event Center

South Royal Brougham Way

STADIUM

Safeco Field

S Atlantic Street

Pike Place Market

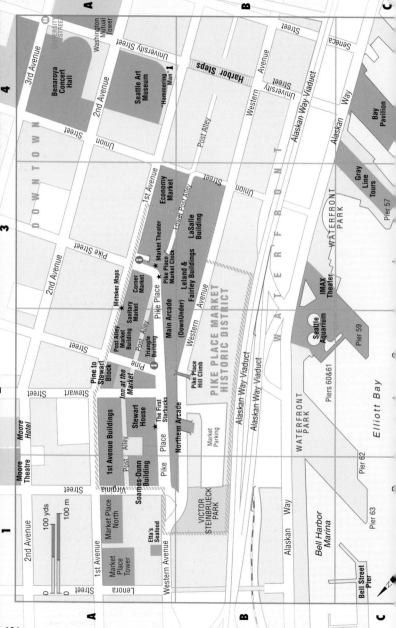

Selective Index for Street Atlas

PLACES OF INTEREST

STREETS

HOTELS

Index

141

Insight Smart Guide: Seattle
Written by: **Helen Townsend**
Edited by: **Joanna Potts**
Proofread and indexed by: **Neil Titman**
Photography by: **APA Tim Thompson** 5B, 5BL, 5MR, 7B, 9B, 9T, 11T, 13B, 13T, 17B, 17T, 21T, 24/25, 26B, 28/29, 28BL, 28BR, 29B, 30B, 30T, 31B, 32/33, 32B, 33B, 34/35, 34BL, 34BR, 35/36, 35B, 36BL, 37B, 38B, 39B, 39T, 40B, 40T, 42/43, 43B, 44/45, 54/55, 54B, 56/57, 65BL, 56BR, 57BL, 57BR, 74/75, 84/85, 87B, 90B, 91B, 94/95, 96T, 97T, 100/101, 100B, 101, 106, 107, 108, 109B, 109T, 112/113, 116BL, 116BR, 117, 118B, 119, 121BL, 121BR, 126/127, 126BL, 126BR, 127B; **APA Jerry Dennis** 4B, 5TL, 11B, 12B, 15T, 15B, 23B, 23T, 26/27, 45B, 47B, 48, 50M, 50T, 51T, 55B, 58B, 60, 61B, 63BL, 61BR, 72, 73, 76/77, 76L, 76R, 77BL, 77BR, 78B, 78T, 79L, 79R, 80, 81, 82B, 83B, 86B, 89B, 94B, 95B, 96B, 98/99, 98B, 99BL, 99BR, 103, 104, 118T, 120/121, 124B; **Alamy** 102; **Fotolibra** 128–9; **Istockphoto** 2/3, 2B, 3T, 5MM, 5TR, 19B, 21B,

27BL, 27BR, 42B, 61T, 68, 70, 86/87, 92/93, 105BL, 105BR, 105T; **PA Photos** 75; **Rex Features** 74B

Cover pictures by: **Getty**
Picture Manager: **Steven Lawrence**
Maps: **James Macdonald/ Mapping Ideas Ltd**
Series Editor: **Jason Mitchell**

First Edition 2009
© 2009 Apa Publications GmbH & Co. Verlag KG Singapore Branch, Singapore.
Printed in Singapore by Insight Print Services (Pte) Ltd

Worldwide distribution enquiries:
Apa Publications GmbH & Co. Verlag KG (Singapore Branch) 38 Joo Koon Road, Singapore 628990; tel: (65) 6865 1600; fax: (65) 6861 6438

Distributed in the UK and Ireland by:
GeoCenter International Ltd
Meridian House, Churchill Way West, Basingstoke, Hampshire RG21 6YR; tel: (44 1256) 817 987; fax: (44 1256) 817 988

Distributed in the United States by:
Langenscheidt Publishers, Inc.
36–36 33rd Street 4th Floor, Long Island City, New York 11106; tel: (1 718) 784 0055; fax: (1 718) 784 0640l

Contacting the Editors
We would appreciate it if readers would alert us to errors or outdated information by writing to:
Apa Publications, PO Box 7910, London SE1 1WE, UK; fax: (44 20) 7403 0290; e-mail: insight@apaguide.co.uk